W9-AZD-101

BROCK LESNAR
The Making of a Hard-Core Legend

By Joel Rippel

TRIUMPH
BOOKS

Library of Congress Cataloging-in-Publication Data TK
Rippel, Joel A., 1956–
    Brock Lesnar : the making of a hard-core legend / by Joel Rippel.
        p. cm.
    Includes bibliographical references.
    ISBN 978-1-60078-381-4
    1. Lesnar, Brock. 2. Wrestlers—United States—Biography. I. Title.
    GV1196.L47R57 2010
    796.812092—dc22
    [B]

                                                        2010027055

This book is available in quantity at special discounts for your group or organization. For further information, contact:
    Triumph Books
    542 South Dearborn Street
    Suite 750
    Chicago, Illinois 60605
    (312) 939–3330
    Fax (312) 663–3557
    www.triumphbooks.com

Printed in U.S.A.

ISBN: 978-1-60078-381-4

Design by Amy Carter

For Preston, who reminds me
that the future is filled with opportunities.

"One of the things Brock had said stuck with me, and I say it to a lot of people. He said, 'You know everybody had the same opportunity to go in the weight room as I did. They just chose not to do it.' You know, so what he did he chose to go in and do something himself, you know, he obviously had a base to build it, but he went in and put in the time and effort and he was reaping awards. People just want to [think]...have a tendency to [think]...he took a shortcut. He didn't take a shortcut. I think that's the thing that stands out."

— J Robinson
Lesnar's wrestling coach
at the University of
Minnesota

CONTENTS

CHAPTER 1

INTRODUCTION

University of Minnesota wrestling coach J Robinson has been observing college wrestling as an athlete, assistant coach, and head coach for 40 years. He has coached Minnesota to three NCAA team championships, and in 2005 he was inducted into the National Wrestling Hall of Fame. So, he is certainly qualified to speak about the sport.

Asked about Brock Lesnar, Robinson said heavyweights like Lesnar are rare.

"People like Brock only come around every 15 or 20 years," Robinson said in a 2009 interview. "You just don't see them. I'm trying to think, all the years. There was a guy at Oklahoma State back in the '60s by the name of Joe James who was just a big physical specimen everybody talked about. But you don't see them very often. They are few and far between when they come."

The reason heavyweights like James and Lesnar are so uncommon is simple.

"They don't come around a lot because most of those guys are playing football," Robinson said. "Look how massive [Brock] is and athletic. Most of those guys that big and athletic have gone where the money is."

Having Lesnar at heavyweight for two years was a luxury for Robinson and the Gophers.

"[Heavyweight] is one of easier weights to win points for at the national tournament," Robinson said, "you know, because there aren't as many good heavyweights. If you can get a pretty good heavyweight, an athletic heavyweight, you can use him to get points there. Just because the majority of the guys aren't athletic."

While wrestling for the Gophers, Lesnar reached the NCAA heavyweight championship match both years and helped the Gophers to a second-place and third-place finish at the NCAA meet.

During his two years at the University of Minnesota, Lesnar went from an unheralded junior college heavyweight to an NCAA champion.

"Here's this young kid, this farm kid from South Dakota," Robinson said, "[who] just basically wanted to go back home and work at the power station, that's all he wanted, get a degree and go back and work at the power station and live on the farm. That's what he wanted to do, get his degree and go back home, and that's the life he saw for himself. But he developed himself, then—as a result of that development, there [are] doors that have been opened to him. It goes back to what he said, 'Everybody had the same chance to go in the weight room as I did, they just chose not to.'

"I think the other thing that happened is that he was very fortunate at a specific time, there was a lot of things going on. I mean, he picked a time; he came along at a very unique time [in] the University of Minnesota's history. Minnesota was coming to the forefront, beating Iowa in the Big Ten. The exposure that he got was way beyond what he could have got anywhere else. In fact, my wife was the marketing director, and we did a lot of PR stuff around him. He had one deal in the paper where [Gophers 141-pounder Chad] Erickson and [Gophers 125-pounder Leroy] Vega were sitting on his shoulders. And they had a big, huge poster designed that showed what his measurements were. I think they had another thing...she [Robinson's wife] came up with,

Introduction

'Brockfast of Champions.' A play on so many things that brought him so much exposure. And then how the team did just kind of amplified it."

Robinson continued, "You know he was part of the catalyst in 2000 and in 1999 for us to win the Big Ten. And that's the year we unseated Iowa. We got to the national tournament and we have a chance to win it. You know, so there's a lot of...you have an upstart program that's rivaling the power to be, and not only that, it's not a California school and a Iowa school, it's Iowa and Minnesota. There's a border mentality between the two already. And then you have two coaches [Robinson and Iowa coach Dan Gable] that coached with each other, so there's just a lot of things that I think brought a lot of exposure to him. He handled it well. And it just kind of fed into all those things that helped him to open some doors."

Several months after the end of his college wrestling career, Lesnar signed with the World Wrestling Federation.

"Here I was wondering how I was going to buy myself a beer and steak after the national tournament, reaching down and pulling out lint," Lesnar recalled to the *Minneapolis Star Tribune* in July 2009. "It was pretty easy. Go with a sure thing. And the sure thing at the time was becoming a pro wrestler."

Lesnar quickly became a star in the WWF. After a stint with Ohio Valley Wrestling, the WWF's development program based in Louisville, Kentucky, Lesnar made his WWF debut in 2002. He was dubbed "The Next Big Thing," and within the year he became the youngest heavyweight champion (at age 25) in WWF history.

But less than two years later, unhappy with physical demands of the business, Lesnar left professional wrestling.

In March 2009, *Sports Illustrated's* L. Jon Wertheim wrote that for Lesnar the "prearranged outcomes in WWE were frustrating."

Lesnar told Wertheim, "I'd put on the best damn show I could, and that's where the competition came from. If I couldn't beat you, I wanted to outperform you. But that gets old."

Lesnar, who had gotten a tattoo on his chest of a knife pointing at his neck, said the schedule got old, too.

"At first I enjoyed it, but I wasn't born to be a pro wrestler," Lesnar told Wertheim. "You spread yourself so thin, you end up bitter."

"I wasn't born to be a pro wrestler."
—Brock Lesnar

In an interview with *UFC Magazine* in December 2009, Lesnar said, "There's an old saying in the entertainment business: 'It's all fake but the money and the miles.'"

Dan Wetzel of Yahoo! Sports wrote in November 2009, "The WWE [which had changed its name from WWF] has a long, ugly history of pushing its wrestlers to cut corners and compete at all costs. Dozens of pro wrestlers have died young, even in their 20s and 30s. Others have pointed to a culture of steroids [Lesnar has denied ever taking them], painkillers, and substance abuse. Whatever the reason, Lesnar did what few do. He walked away."

Figure Four Weekly, a wrestling newsletter, recapped Lesnar's WWE career. "The rest is history. Brock signed, he progressed fairly well in OVW though not to the level of a Kurt Angle, he was arguably brought up too early, and then when he got a huge push right out of the gate and the chance to work every night with high-level workers, he improved at an almost alarming rate. By the end of his short career, he had become one of the best big-man workers ever to step foot into a wrestling ring."

After trying out with the Minnesota Vikings in the fall of 2004, Lesnar wrestled briefly in Japan and had a long legal battle with the WWE.

In 2006, Lesnar began training in mixed martial arts. After his first Mixed Martial Arts (MMA) fight in 2007, Lesnar became interested in joining the Ultimate Fighting Championship (UFC).

Introduction

His junior college wrestling coach had suggested the UFC to Lesnar ten years earlier.

"The funny thing is," said Bruce Basaraba, who was co-coach of the Bismarck (North Dakota) State College wrestling team, "during one of his two years in Bismarck, North Dakota State came to Bismarck Civic Center to wrestle Nebraska. Nebraska had a couple of guys from Bismarck. Before we went down to the dual, I had our team over for dinner and to watch a little TV. The UFC was on and I said to Brock, 'You know, Brock, you should go into that.'"

In the December 2009 issue of *UFC Magazine*, Lesnar said he had "watched the first UFC, and I was a fan. Thing about this...it was different and guys like Royce Gracie and Dan Serven were actually doing this and making a living off it. It was intriguing. I didn't have an inkling that I could compete until I started competing. I knew that I had a great mentality, and I knew that I'd been in enough fights. You've got to understand that you can't just jump into the sport if you don't have a true wrestling background."

Wetzel wrote that Lesnar approached UFC president Dana White and said, "Let me fight. Give me one chance." White's response, according to Wetzel was, "It's no job for on-the-job training."

Lesnar replied, "I'm either good at this or I'm not."

In an interview with *Maxim* magazine in the spring of 2009, Lesnar recalled his sales pitch to White. "There's not another fighter in the UFC [who] looks like me. [Who] has the star power that I've got. I'm known all over the world because I was a pro wrestler. I've been to 30 different countries that know my name. I put asses in the seats, and I sell pay-per-views."

Despite a loss to Frank Mir in his first UFC fight, Lesnar quickly showed that he was good at it. In just his third UFC fight, he won the UFC heavyweight championship. In his fourth fight, he avenged his loss to Mir by defeating Mir to retain the heavyweight title.

But before his next title defense—as part of UFC 106 in November

2009—Lesnar's career was interrupted when he was hospitalized with an illness that threatened his career. In early 2010, after several months of uncertainty, it was announced that Lesnar was on the road to recovery and ready to resume his UFC career.

CHAPTER 2

GROWING UP IN WEBSTER, SOUTH DAKOTA

Living on a dairy farm is hard work, and it helped Brock Lesnar develop his work ethic at an early age. By the time he was five years old, he'd suffered two hernias helping his father, Rich, on the family farm just outside of Webster, South Dakota.

Richard Lesnar, Brock's father, said in an interview on the 2003 WWE-produced DVD *Here Comes the Pain* that his son was, "Very independent, very headstrong, liked to be outdoors, even at the age of four and five he wanted to help on the farm. He was really a worker."

Brock's mother, Stephanie, said on the DVD, "Brock Edward Lesnar, he weighed 9 [pounds] 9 [ounces], and they called him pork-chops. Brock was robust, on the go, inquisitive." Brock was the youngest of three sons. Brock's oldest brother, Troy, is eight years older than Brock. Chad Lesnar is six years older than Brock. Both Troy and Chad played football in high school. Chad also wrestled in high school.

At the age of five, Brock developed an interest in the sport that would define him.

Lesnar told *UFC Magazine* in late 2009, "From a really young age, I was a physical kid who enjoyed physical contact. I started wrestling when I was five years old. My older brothers fought a lot. It was just part of living in a small town, I guess. It was one of those things to do on the weekend. I was always scrapping.

"We had rivalry towns because of sports. Or just because we were chasing some girls and the guys didn't like us. I guess it's all about territory. You could say I went out looking for fights on the weekends. And looking back, it wasn't right. Nowadays, kids have an escape to get out this sort of thing, take their aggression out at the gym."

Lesnar's hometown of Webster was located in northeastern South Dakota in the heart of a glacial lakes area known for pheasant hunting and fishing. The town, which was founded in the mid-1880s after the railroad reached South Dakota, is the county seat of Day County. The county has 1,061 square miles—91 percent of which is farmland.

The county's population peaked at 15,194 in 1920. By 1980, three years after Brock Lesnar was born, the county's population was 8,100. In the 2000 U.S. Census, the county's population was 6,267. Webster's population in 2000 was 1,952.

The community of Webster has produced a governor of South Dakota (Sigurd Anderson), a network television anchorman (Tom Brokaw), and an executive of Major League Baseball (Laurel Prieb).

Brock Lesnar described his youth in Webster on the *Here Comes the Pain* DVD:

"A rural farm community, lots of grain farms. I grew up on a dairy farm. We used to have about 200 head of cows. I left here in 1996, used to have some good times here and some hard times. It was just kind of backwoodsy, kind of out in the country, not a lot going on. Everybody knows everybody and everybody knows everybody's business.

"I was a very aggressive young kid, eager to do anything, always up for any challenges. I would always like to do the regular farm kid stuff. Some nights it would just be cool to sleep up in the hay loft. My hay loft was like my jungle gym. As a young kid, I was a real tall, lean, skinny kid. I was very limber and strong. I was always active; I was always doing push-ups, always doing sit-ups, always working out as long as I can remember.

"I discovered sports at a very young age. My high school and little kid wrestling coach, I grew up two miles from him. He took me under his wing and guided me to wrestle. He saw some potential in me at a very young age; I started to wrestle when I was like five or six."

Lesnar's mentor was John Schiley, the Webster High School wrestling coach. Schiley helped Lesnar focus on sports just as Webster wrestling coach Chuck Scheppy had helped Schiley while he was growing up in Webster. Scheppy coached the Bearcats to four state Class B titles and one runner-up finish in a six-year span from 1974–79.

According to Webster native Laurel Prieb, vice president for western operations and special projects for Major League Baseball, Scheppy was a "dynamic coach."

Prieb told the *Minneapolis Star Tribune* that he was entering junior high when Scheppy turned Webster into a "wrestling powerhouse. His wrestlers had a passion, a devotion, a love for Scheppy that was amazing. If he had told them...I don't know, 'Go plow up the golf course and plant corn,' they would have done it. The wrestlers practiced in a dingy room with a low ceiling. It was 112 degrees in there, I swear."

Wrestling for Scheppy, Schiley won three state titles—at 98 pounds in 1973 and at 105 pounds in 1974 and 1975. Schiley, whose family owned a hog farm three miles from the Lesnar's farm, became the Webster wrestling coach in 1986. Schiley had spent the previous five years as the coach of the Webster youth wrestling program.

"We [Schiley and his assistant LeeRon Paszek] want to help because we got something out of the program when we were in school and want to put something back in," Schiley told the *Webster Reporter and Farmer*.

Schiley told the newspaper that his first year as head coach was a struggle.

"The team scored only seven points at the regional and one of those was taken away for unsportsmanlike conduct by one of the athletes. [Only] one wrestler advanced to the state tourney. I almost gave up after the first year!"

But Schiley stayed and gradually restored the program to prominence. Even though he had been a successful high school and college wrestler (a three-time all-conference wrestler for Huron College), Schiley didn't impose a wrestling style on his athletes, telling the *Reporter and Farmer*, "That doesn't work. None of the kids reflect our styles. They've developed their own styles."

One thing Schiley's squads did reflect was his intensity.

"I'm known for being the yellingest coach in the state," Schiley told the *Reporter and Farmer* in the mid-1990s. "I call it emotionally motivating them from the sidelines. The kids pretty much know what they are capable of. Sometimes they need a little extra motivation from the sidelines to get a pin. We try to wear down our opponents. By the third period, they're ours. We've never lost a match in overtime. I think that speaks for itself.

"The kids that are wrestling now nearly all came through the youth wrestling program from sophomore on down. It's tough on me as a coach running both [high school and youth] programs, but it gives consistency all the way through."

Schiley said the key to his coaching was communication.

"Maybe it's a little more difficult to be a coach because I have to worry about 13 kids. When I wrestled I just worried about myself," Schiley told the newspaper. "We tell the kids we're not having them do anything we didn't do. It takes a special individual to be in the championship bracket at the state tournament. Before each match we talk with the team about each wrestler's job. Sometimes it's to get a pin; sometimes it's to win; sometimes it's just to wrestle so the team won't have to give up a forfeit. We also compliment the kids, which is something people don't always see us doing. This system seems to work pretty well."

Lesnar, who had started working on his wrestling skills while still in grade school, joined the Webster wrestling team as a seventh-grader.

"Brock has worked for me on the farm for most of his life," Schiley told the *Minneapolis Star Tribune* in 1999. "He was always a big eater, always loved milk. My mother used to cook lunch for us when we were working at the farm. There was a roast for Brock, a gallon of milk for Brock, and a roast and gallon of milk for the rest of us. Brock was my 105-pounder in the seventh and eighth grade, then he started going up five weight classes per year. He was skinny, with very long legs. He grew tall before he grew large. He was an ugly, deformed-looking creature to be honest."

Schiley brought Lesnar along slowly.

On the *Here Comes the Pain* DVD, Lesnar recalled, "I can remember going in and just having an attitude. I thought I was pretty bad, still do today. I don't have many highlights as an amateur wrestler; the only thing I can remember is people being scared to wrestle me because I was very physical. Maybe I didn't win all the time, but one thing was for sure—if you were wrestling me, you were going to get beat up, because that's what it is, it's just one on one, it's basically a legal street fight with a few rules. That's what I liked about it."

Schiley described Lesnar's development as a wrestler on the *Here Comes the Pain* DVD. "He was always a strength wrestler but lots of times he didn't have the strength to wrestle that way, so he got defeated here and there. He always had a little bit of a temper and was very aggressive. From early on we found that he couldn't cut weight very well, because every time we had him cut weight he didn't make weight, then he got really ornery. So we just decided that he was going to be a big guy and kept feeding him.

"I believe you have to learn to lose before you learn to win, and Brock lost his share of matches and he was not special coming up in the kid's ranks, and then he caught on. And once Brock gets confidence in doing something, he's unbeatable."

There were some highlights for Lesnar in his first varsity season.

On January 4, 1991, wrestling at 119 pounds, Lesnar contributed to Webster's victory over Aberdeen Roncalli with a 12–6 decision over Greg Holland. Later in the month, Lesnar pinned Britton's Cory Bremmon in 5:10 to help Webster earn a 52–14 victory.

On February 3, the Bearcats lost to Clark, which was ranked No. 3 in the South Dakota Class B state poll. Wrestling at 125 pounds, Lesnar was pinned, but the *Webster Reporter and Farmer* reported, "Schiley also singled out Brock Lesnar for his efforts during the dual. Lesnar, a seventh grader, was up against a senior."

That was likely Lesnar's last varsity action of the season. The Bearcats traveled to Britton on February 9, where they finished third at the District 1B tournament. Eleven Bearcats, including three champions, qualified to the Regional 1B tournament. At the regional tournament, held in Groton on February 16, the Bearcats finished third and qualified seven wrestlers—their most since 1981—for the state meet.

On February 23, at Huron, the Bearcats finished ninth at the State Class B meet. Northeastern Conference rival Redfield won the meet.

Going into the 1991–92 season, Lesnar was one of 10 returning lettermen for the Bearcats. The Bearcats had lost just three seniors from the previous season's squad, which had an 11–6 dual-meet record.

Schiley was optimistic about the squad. In the team's season preview in the December 2, 1991, issue of the *Reporter and Farmer*, he said, "We'll take it slow and steady in our climb to the top. We've got a quality team. We've got a lot of experience, especially because six of them wrestled almost year-round last year."

The Bearcats opened the season at a quadrangular on December 5. Both the Bearcats and Lesnar, wrestling at 125, went 2–1. In the

Bearcats' 46–25 victory over Deuel, Lesnar won by forfeit. In the Bearcats' 46–20 loss to Madison, Lesnar was pinned in 1:43. Lesnar regrouped to pin his opponent in 2:29 in the Bearcats' 54–21 victory over Plankinton.

The following week, the *Reporter and Farmer* reported that there would be a meeting on December 19 for the parents of Webster youth and high school wrestlers to discuss new diets and for a presentation on the "dos and don'ts" of parenting.

Lesnar was still being brought along slowly and was in and out of the Bearcats' lineup.

In late January, six of the top 10 teams in the state Class B poll gathered at the Parkston Tournament. Lesnar, wrestling at 130 pounds, went 2–1 at the tournament, losing by pin in his first match before winning 13–4 and 6–0.

Schiley told the *Reporter and Farmer*, "This was like a mini-state tourney. We had some tough matches."

The Bearcats, who had seven wrestlers ranked at their weight in the state Class B individual rankings, finished second (to Hamlin) in the district meet on February 15 in Clark. A week later, the Bearcats played host to the regional meet, where they finished second to Hamlin again. At the state meet in Aberdeen, the Bearcats finished 12th.

Schiley told the *Reporter and Farmer* that he was already looking forward to next season.

"This team has learned to win and with 14 good freshmen [including Lesnar] coming in next season, we look forward to a higher finish," Schiley said.

The Bearcats went into the 1992–93 season—Lesnar's freshman year—with 14 returning lettermen among the 34 wrestlers who went out for the team. Schiley thought the Bearcats could be one of the top teams in the Northeast Conference.

The Bearcats opened the season on December 3 with a 40–27 victory over Deuel. Lesnar got his season off to a good start by pinning his opponent in 1:49. The *Reporter and Farmer* recapped the meet by saying, "Brock Lesnar, who weighs about 143 pounds, wrestled in the 152-pound weight class and pinned his opponent."

Schiley told the newspaper, "I wondered if he should have been wrestling in that weight class. I was impressed by him."

Two days later, the Bearcats wrestled in the Clark Tournament. The Bearcats went 1–3, losing their first three matches before defeating Northwestern in the seventh-place match. Lesnar went 3–1 on the day, with the three victories at 145 pounds coming by forfeit. Wrestling at 152 pounds in the Bearcats' 60–12 loss to host Clark in the second round, Lesnar was pinned in 0:59.

On December 21, the Bearcats went 1–2 at the Watertown Invitational. In his only match of the day, Lesnar was pinned in 1:18 in the Bearcats' 34–30 loss to Madison.

One week later, the Bearcats, ranked No. 5 in the state Class B poll, played host to the Northeast Conference meet. The Bearcats finished second to Milbank and had 10 wrestlers finish in the top four in their individual weight classes. Lesnar did not wrestle.

The Bearcats began the new year with eight consecutive dual-meet victories. On January 5, the Bearcats went 3–0 at the Britton Quadrangular. Lesnar lost his first match of the day 11–8 but won his next two matches by pin (in 1:29 and 4:18).

Schiley told the Webster newspaper, "It was a good night. Every wrestler had one or two wins, and everyone had a chance to wrestle."

On January 9, the Bearcats played host to Redfield and Madison. In the Bearcats' 44–15 victory over Redfield, Lesnar was pinned by Josh Kimlicka. The Bearcats then edged Madison 29–28, but Lesnar suffered a 5–2 loss to Nathan Moore.

Three days later, the Bearcats wrestled three duals at the Hamlin Quadrangular. Lesnar didn't wrestle as the Bearcats defeated host Hamlin 54–14. In the Bearcats' 66–0 victory over Sioux Valley, Lesnar won with an 11–2 major decision. He followed that with a victory by pin (in 1:00) in the Bearcats' 57–9 victory over the Flandreau Indian School.

On January 16, the Bearcats traveled 160 miles to Gettysburg where they won the 13-team Gettysburg Invitational with 242 points. Host Gettysburg-Hoven was a distant second with 119.5 points. Lesnar started his day with two victories—by pin (in 0:37) and by major decision (10–0). But he lost each of his next two matches by pin (in 0:35 and 0:50).

On January 20, the Bearcats easily defeated Aberdeen Roncalli (67–4) and DeSmet (63–6). After sitting out the victory over Roncalli, Lesnar defeated DeSmet's Wade Brendan 16–11.

"He's the most improved wrestler on the team at this point."
—Coach Schiley

Three days later, the Bearcats competed in the Parkston Little B Tournament. The Bearcats won the 10-team tournament with 175 points. Stanley County was second with 147.5 points. Lesnar went 2–2 on the day. He won his first-round match 9–3 before suffering a loss by pin (in 1:20) in the second round. He rebounded to win by pin (in 2:07) before losing to Hamlin's Warren Ingalls 4–1 in the third-place match.

Lesnar's performance at Parkston earned praise from his coach. Schiley told the *Reporter and Farmer*, "Brock had his best tourney yet. I'd consider a freshman at 152 pounds a success because he's usually wrestling juniors or seniors. He's the most improved wrestler on the team at this point."

Lesnar lost his next three matches—10–8 in the Bearcats' 42–16 victory over Clark, by pin (in 5:53) in the Bearcats' 52–10 loss to Milbank, and 12–4 in the Bearcats' 50–13 victory over Sisseton.

In the Bearcats' next dual meet, a 60–5 victory over Doland-Conde, Lesnar won by forfeit.

The Bearcats ended the regular season on February 6 on a positive note, winning the 10-team Britton Invitational with 204 points. Ellendale (North Dakota) was second with 159 points. Lesnar had a first-round bye before winning his second-round match by pin (in 5:04). In the 152-pound championship match, Lesnar suffered a loss by pin (in 1:30).

"We found out we can wrestle three days in a row," Schiley told the *Reporter and Farmer*, after the Bearcats had wrestled one dual on Thursday and two duals on Friday before competing in the Britton Tournament on Saturday.

The Bearcats, who were still ranked No. 5 in the state Class B poll, and Lesnar, who compiled an 18–13 record in the regular season, were ready for the district tournament.

On February 13, the Bearcats won the district title with 181.5 points—32.5 points more than the runner-up—as Lesnar earned his first district title. After a bye in the first round, Lesnar outlasted Wade Brendan, who he had defeated by a 16–11 decision earlier in the season, 6–5. In the 152-pound championship match, Lesnar pinned Clark's Darin Anderson in 3:50. Anderson had pinned Lesnar in 59 seconds in the first week of the season.

Lesnar was one of five district champions for the Bearcats, who advanced all 12 wrestlers to the regional meet.

On February 20, the Bearcats made the 90-mile trip to Redfield for the region meet. It was a successful day for the Bearcats, who earned their first region title in 14 years with 150.5 points. Deuel (122.5 points) was second, and host Redfield (116.5 points) was third.

Lesnar was the runner-up at 152 pounds to earn his first state-meet berth. Lesnar won his first-round match, 9–5, before losing by pin (in 0:28) in the second round. He outlasted Jeremy Schafer of Deuel 8–7 to earn a shot at the region title. In the championship match, he was pinned by Highmore's J.D. Anderson in 1:51.

On February 26 in Watertown, the first day of the two-day state meet, Lesnar went 0–2 with both losses coming by pin.

"Friday was a bad night," Schiley told the *Reporter and Farmer*. "We ran into some real strong kids."

On the second day of the meet, the Bearcats went on to finish in eighth place. A highlight for the Bearcats was a championship by Casey Sichmeller at 103 pounds. Sichmeller was Webster's first state champion in 10 years.

As a sophomore in the fall of 1993, Lesnar joined the Bearcats' varsity football team. Lesnar lettered as a lineman as the Bearcats went 5–4 overall and 4–3 in the Northeast Conference. The Bearcats' season ended with a first-round playoff loss to Clark.

With six returning state-meet qualifiers among 12 returning lettermen, the Bearcats wrestling team had lofty goals for the 1993–94 season.

The season preview in the November 29 issue of the *Reporter and Farmer* was headlined, "State Title is Goal of Wrestling Team." Others expected a lot of the Bearcats, too—the team was ranked No. 1 in the state Class B preseason poll.

The Bearcats opened Lesnar's sophomore season on December 2 with a 48–21 victory over Deuel. Lesnar aided the victory by winning by pin at 160 pounds.

On December 11, the Bearcats went 3–1 at the Watertown Tournament—defeating Sioux Falls Roosevelt (43–21), Sioux Falls O'Gorman (48–18), and Sioux Falls Washington (41–21) before losing to Milbank (45–6). Lesnar went 2–2 on the day, winning a 6–5 decision and by pin (in 4:38) before dropping 9–7 and 3–1 decisions. The 3–1 loss was to Milbank's Jason Ehlebracht, who had pinned Lesnar in 5:53 the previous season.

On December 21, Webster won twice—defeating DeSmet (67–3) and Arlington (41–25)—as Lesnar went 1–1, winning 14–5 and losing 8–5.

Two days after Christmas, the Bearcats won the Northeast Conference tournament for the first time in 18 years. Ironically, despite the conference championship, the Bearcats dropped from No. 1 to No. 3 in the next state Class B poll.

Lesnar went 2–2 at the conference meet. After a first-round bye, Lesnar suffered another tough loss to Ehlebracht, who held on for a 1–0 victory. He then won by pin (in 2:13) and by a 7–0 decision. In the match for third place, he lost to Redfield's Josh Kimlicka 6–0. The previous season, Kimlicka pinned Lesnar in 3:40.

The January 3, 1994, issue of the *Reporter and Farmer* carried an interesting story headlined, "Martial Arts Popular Here." The Webster Community Education Program offered classes in martial arts. Randy Becking, who had won state wrestling championships for Webster in 1978 and 1979, was the instructor.

In mid-January, the Bearcats defeated Hamlin, Redfield, and Madison in duals. Lesnar was just 1–2 in those three duals, but his victory was 5–3 decision over Kimlicka, whom he had lost to at the conference meet.

Schiley told the *Reporter and Farmer* his team was improving, "We challenge our kids every week. We're more consistent. It makes us tougher. The kids are getting better."

Between January 15 and January 22, the Bearcats won two invitational tournaments and won two dual meets. The Bearcats opened that stretch by finishing in first place at the 13-team Gettysburg Tournament. Lesnar won the 160-pound title with three impressive victories—two by pin (in 2:33 and in 3:49) and one by major decision (15–4).

On January 20, the Bearcats routed Aberdeen Roncalli (65–3) and Northwestern (70–0) as Lesnar earned two victories—by pin (in 4:24) and by forfeit.

Two days later, the Bearcats won the 11-team Parkston Tournament as Lesnar went 2–1. He opened with a major-decision victory (14–2), but suffered a loss by pin (in 1:29). He finished the day with a 6–1 victory.

The Bearcats and Lesnar finished the regular season strong—the Bearcats won three duals and took first in the nine-team Britton Invitational as Lesnar went 4–1. Lesnar won the 160-pound title at the Britton Tournament with a pin (in 0:38) and a 12–3 major decision.

On February 12, the Bearcats played host to the district tournament and successfully defended their district title. Lesnar took third at 160, winning the third-place match by pin (in 2:23).

A week later, the Bearcats defended their regional title by qualifying 10 wrestlers for the state meet. Lesnar qualified for his second state meet with a third-place finish at 160 pounds.

At the state Class B meet in Aberdeen, Lesnar suffered a first-round loss by pin (in 2:31). Lesnar came back to win his first match in the wrestlebacks, 10–2, but his second state meet came to an end with a 6–1 loss in the wrestlebacks second round.

The Bearcats finished in second place—their best finish at the state meet since 1983—with 107.5 points, seven points behind first-place Wagner.

In the season recap, Schiley told the *Reporter and Farmer* that despite the Bearcats' success in the 1993–94 season, there was "a missing ingredient. I'm talking about the tragic accident that claimed the life of [a Webster] seventh-grade wrestler. The tragedy [which happened the previous summer] brought us together, and the team dedicated the season to [the wrestler] and his family."

Lesnar began his junior year of high school as one of 12 returning lettermen on the Bearcats football team. Lesnar was expected to be a two-way starter for the Bearcats—in the offensive line and at nose guard on defense.

"We were really hurt by graduation, losing 12 seniors, eight of whom started on offense and defense," Bearcats coach Randy Pirner told the *Reporter and Farmer*. "It is tough with a big loss like that, but we are experienced at the skilled positions and are hoping our young linemen will come along quickly. The players have been really focused in practice, and I expect this to be a fun team to coach."

The Bearcats opened the season on September 2 with a 14–6 loss to Mobridge. A week later, the Bearcats lost to Deuel, 6–0. Pirner told the *Reporter and Farmer* after the loss to Deuel, "The kids played a tremendously hard-hitting game," and noted that Lesnar (along with Scott Kulesa and Jason Nolte) were defensive standouts.

The Bearcats defense played well again the next week—with seven sacks—in a 14–0 victory over Hamlin.

On September 23, Lesnar had a team-high 12 tackles to lead the Bearcats to their second consecutive victory—23–0 over Redfield. On September 30, Kulesa had 13 tackles and Lesnar had 11 tackles to lead the Bearcats to a 16–6 victory over Milbank.

Pirner told the *Reporter and Farmer* that the victory over Milbank was a "big emotional win. We needed it to go to 3–2, it was homecoming and it gives us a boost going into the [Aberdeen] Roncalli game."

But the Bearcats' three-game winning streak came to an end the next week in a 25–6 loss to Roncalli.

On October 14, the Bearcats used a stifling defense to defeat Groton 25–0. Groton managed only 22 yards in total offense—23 yards passing and minus-1 yards rushing.

The Bearcats closed out the regular season on October 21 with a 21–13 loss to Clark. Lesnar led the Bearcats with nine tackles. On October 27, the Bearcats season came to an end with a 13–6 first-round playoff loss to Deuel.

Pirner told the *Reporter and Farmer*, "All we needed was a play here or a play there, but it didn't happen. It has been like that most of the season, and the kids and I came away from this game very frustrated. When taking a closer look at it, though, we were very competitive in one of the most balanced conferences and regions in the state this season."

Even with a solid nucleus of 11 returning lettermen, the Bearcats wrestling team had some question marks going into Lesnar's junior season.

"We have a number of good kids back," Schiley told the *Reporter and Farmer*, "but injuries to upperweight wrestlers Kenny Foshiem and Jason Nolte will put some extra pressure on us in early matches. We'll have trouble matching up at some weights because several younger athletes will be going against juniors and seniors. We have the opportunity to be a good team this season, but we need to avoid injuries, have some leaders step forward...and several of our younger wrestlers will have to perform well."

The injury to Nolte had a big impact on Lesnar. An article in the *Minneapolis Star Tribune* a few years later described the event. "The two [Nolte and Lesnar] were wrestling and football teammates who had a mutual dislike. That changed after a playoff football game in which Lesnar and Nolte collided trying to tackle a ball carrier. Nolte ended up with broken vertebrae in his neck. He wasn't paralyzed, but he did miss the wrestling season."

Lesnar recalled in the article, "After the game, I went to see him. I felt like I had taken something away from him."

After Nolte recovered from the injury, he and Lesnar started training together, which motivated Lesnar to go to the gym every day.

For his junior season, Lesnar, who had wrestled at 160 pounds as a sophomore, was moving up to 189 pounds.

The season got off to a disappointing start for Lesnar. In the Bearcats' season-opening 41–14 victory over Deuel on November 29, Lesnar lost to Deuel's Jason Bauman 7–1.

After that dual, the Bearcats had 11 days to prepare for the Watertown Tournament. Schiley told the *Reporter and Farmer* he looked forward to the tournament because it exposed the Class B Bearcats to Class A competition.

"This is always a good tournament for us because of the tough competition early in the season," Schiley said. "It will give us a good idea where we are and where we have to go to compete with better teams in our class."

At the tournament on December 10, the Bearcats went 2–2—defeating Sisseton (43–25) and Sioux Falls Roosevelt (41–29) and losing to Milbank (37–25) and Sioux Falls Washington (36–30). Lesnar rebounded by going 4–0 on the day with three pins and a 9–4 decision.

Five days later the Bearcats tuned up for the Northeast Conference meet by winning three duals—over Arlington (38–18), DeSmet (70–6), and Flandreau (61–6). After a tough 5–3 victory over Arlington's Mike Schultz, Lesnar pinned his next two opponents (in 5:21 and 0:18).

On December 17, Lesnar earned his first conference title to help the Bearcats to a third-place finish (behind first-place Redfield and second place Milbank) at the Northeast Conference meet. Lesnar defeated his first two opponents 10–5 and 12–0 to advance to the championship match, where he won by pin in 68 seconds.

Schiley told the *Reporter and Farmer*, "We didn't wrestle bad, but we didn't wrestle super, either. We need a little more snap and will intensify our holidays with Troy Knebel helping the kids on weights to increase their strength. We only have one senior wrestling right now, so we're young and want to continue to improve."

After the conference meet, the Bearcats had a 16-day break before kicking off the new year on January 3 with victories over Britton (64–3) and Groton (55–15). Lesnar needed less than a minute to pin each opponent.

A week later, the Bearcats traveled to Hamlin where they won three matches—beating Hamlin (39–21), Flandreau (67–8), and DeSmet

(54–18). Lesnar pinned all three of his opponents—in 44 seconds, 9 seconds, and 56 seconds—to give him six consecutive victories by pin.

On January 12, the Bearcats and Lesnar continued to roll with two more victories. The Bearcats defeated Redfield 33–26, getting six crucial points from Lesnar's victory by pin at 189 pounds. The Bearcats also defeated Madison 40–9, as Lesnar contributed an 8–4 victory (ending his consecutive pin streak).

Schiley was pleased with the team's effort against Redfield, telling the *Reporter and Farmer*, "They [Redfield] were rated one step higher than we were in Class B and won [the] conference [meet], so it was great for our kids to knock them off. It was the best effort of the season."

On January 14, the Bearcats took first place at the Gettysburg Tournament, as Lesnar won the 189-pound title. In the final, Lesnar defeated Doland-Conde's Dave Madsen, 8–2. In a 54–14 victory over Aberdeen Roncalli five days later, Lesnar won by pin.

A week later, the Bearcats finished third at the Parkston Tournament behind first-place Stanley County and second-place Parkston (the top ranked team in the state Class B poll). Lesnar won his first two matches convincingly by pin (1:09) and technical fall (16–2), but in the 189-pound final he lost to Parkston's Lance Thiry. The loss ended a 22-match winning streak for Lesnar.

On January 24, Lesnar started a new winning streak with a victory by pin (in 54 seconds) in the Bearcats' 39–18 victory over Sisseton.

One of the regular-season's highlights for Lesnar and the Bearcats came on January 26 when Lesnar, wrestling at heavyweight, played a key role in the Bearcats' 32–24 victory over Milbank.

The Bearcats were clinging to a 26–24 lead going into the heavyweight match. Lesnar sealed the Bearcats' victory with a pin (in 3:09) of Milbank's Josh Bohlen. It was the Bearcats' first dual-meet victory over the Bulldogs in 21 years. Earlier in the season, Milbank had defeated the Bearcats 37–25 at the Watertown Tournament.

In its recap of the victory, the *Reporter and Farmer* wrote, "Brock Lesnar, who has been wrestling at 189 and heavyweight this season, came up with his biggest win of the season."

Schiley told the newspaper, "You have to be excited for the kids. It has been a long time since our wrestlers beat Milbank in a dual, and they are ranked fifth in Class A behind Mitchell, Pierre, Watertown, and Huron. It is the best the kids have wrestled all season. They were really focused and wrestled with intensity."

"They were really focused and wrestled with intensity."
—Coach Schiley

The Bearcats won their final two dual-meets of the season against Clark (38–25) and Doland-Conde (65–9) as Lesnar recorded pins in both matches (in 12 seconds and 4:24). The victories pushed the Bearcats' winning streak to 15 matches and gave them an 18–2 dual-meet record.

They closed out the regular season by taking second place at the Britton Tournament. The Bearcats had 171.5 points—9.5 points behind first-place Faulkton—as Lesnar tuned up for the postseason with two pins (one in 9 seconds) and a 4–2 victory over Doland-Conde's Dave Madsen for the 189-pound title.

After the grueling regular season, Schiley and his assistant coach, LeeRon Paszek, tried an offbeat approach to prepare the team for the district and region tournaments.

Schiley told the *Reporter and Farmer*, "January was a real tough month for the kids with so many matches and traveling. They are burned out, so we decided to try something different before the tourneys."

The day before the district tournament, the coaches played basketball with the team. The next day at Clear Lake, the Bearcats, who were ranked No. 5 in the state Class B poll, responded by winning their third consecutive district title. The Bearcats had 170.5 points to out-distance second-place Clark, which had 112 points.

The Bearcats had six individual champions—including Lesnar—and advanced 11-of-12 wrestlers to the region meet. After a first-round bye, Lesnar won by pin (in 1:32) and then outlasted Deuel's Jason Bauman 3–2 for his second district title (he won his first two years earlier at 152 pounds). Bauman had defeated Lesnar 7–1 in the Bearcats' season-opener on November 29.

"This is the first year since I've been coaching that we didn't have a practice before the district," Schiley told the *Reporter and Farmer*, "But the kids wrestled better in the district than they have all year. Heck, LeeRon and I were relaxed at the district, too, and one coach wanted to know how we could be so calm. I told him 'The team played basketball yesterday, and we're going to play volleyball Friday before the regional—maybe you should give it a try.'

"All the wins were big for the 'Cats at districts, among them Aaron Tvinnereim's win over the unbeaten No. 2 wrestler in the state at 112 pounds [Travous Milton of Deuel] 4–2 in the championship match."

Schiley told the newspaper that when the season started, the team had no definite leader, but many leaders had emerged, "especially junior Brock Lesnar."

Lesnar, who was ranked No. 3 at 189 pounds in the state Class B poll, told the newspaper, "When I first started wrestling, I made a lot of mistakes, but I have learned from them now. I am more intense and can make my moves better. This year's team is a lot more together, and team spirit is shown more."

Sichmeller, who had moved up to 130 pounds, told the newspaper, "Every moment counts out there on the mat. I think the fact [that] we are tough and stubborn will take us a long way."

The newspaper's recap of the district meet noted, "Many of the wrestlers said the reason they wrestle is they love the sport. Many of

"I am more intense and can make my moves better."
—Brock Lesnar

them have been together for 12 years, and they have formed lasting friendships with each other."

Schiley was asked for his prediction on the upcoming regional tournament. He told the newspaper, "The kids have been waiting a year for the tournaments to begin, and at this point in the season, LeeRon and I have done about all we can to get them ready—now it is up to them."

The coach went on to say that he expected the Bearcats, Redfield, Clark, and Deuel to have "the most to say who ended up regional champion. I think the regional will be closer than some people think. We beat Deuel in some key matches at districts, but if they get by some of our kids at regionals, the Cardinals will be right there."

On February 18, in nearby Groton (33 miles due west of Webster), the Bearcats outdueled Redfield for their third consecutive regional title. The Bearcats, who had four individual champions, finished with 135.5 points. Redfield had 124 points.

Lesnar finished second at 189 pounds, winning by pin (in 1:11) and by major decision (9–0) before losing to Bauman, whom he had defeated for the district title, 10–5.

The relaxed Bearcats turned their focus to the state meet.

The *Reporter and Farmer* reported, "The wrestlers enjoyed the change of pace before the pressure-packed tourneys, but Coach John Schiley gave a definite 'no' to a loyal follower of the Cats, who asked him if his grapplers were going to play a little hockey before the State B Tournament at Watertown. 'We might do a little bowling though,' he laughed."

The *Reporter and Farmer* went on to report that Schiley said, "Sometimes coaches and fans can put too much pressure on athletes," and that he was using the philosophy "an 86-year old told him about a horse."

Schiley said the man told him, "All year he used the reins to show the horse where to go, but when he and his mount got caught in a snowstorm, he realized he had to tie the reins up and let the horse find the way home. In a way, that's what we're letting the kids do."

Schiley analyzed the upcoming state meet for the newspaper.

"Some of our kids got tough seeds the first day, and how we perform will have a lot to do with how we finish Saturday night," Schiley said. "I figure we will need at least four kids and a couple of other finishers in third-sixth if we want to be a contender for the team title, but Coach Paszek and I told our kids not to worry about the team title. We just told them to go out and wrestle, have fun, and see what the scoreboard reads on Saturday night. They put together two good tournaments in a row—we'll see what happens this time around."

According to Schiley, even though Parkston and Webster had each qualified eight wrestlers for the state meet, there was no clear-cut favorite for the team title, but that "Bon Homme had four wrestlers who could win a state title. Webster, Howard, Stanley County, Philip, and Redfield [will] have a lot to say about who takes home the championship trophy. [And] Bennett County is a sleeper."

Lesnar took a 33–3 record into his third state meet, which began on February 24 in Watertown. He opened with an 11–0 victory in the first round, but in the quarterfinals he was defeated by Eric Porisch of Flandreau, 6–3.

Lesnar rebounded with three consecutive victories in the wrestlebacks—two by pins (in 2:03 and in 1:29) and one by decision (7–0)—to earn the chance to wrestle for third place. In the third-place match, Lesnar won an 8–2 decision over Porisch. Porisch had lost in the semifinals after defeating Lesnar in the quarterfinals.

As a team, the Bearcats finished third as Bon Homme earned its first state title.

"I said before the tournament that if we won third or better, it would be a good tournament for us," Schiley told the *Reporter and Farmer*, "and as it turned out, we had our chances at second place, even though Corey Johnson wasn't able to wrestle because of an injured shoulder.

"Before the tourney, I pegged Bon Homme as a team with five good wrestlers who could win it—and they did with 113.5 points, crowning three champions. I also had Parkston figured as a contender, and they took second with 90 points, while we totaled 78.5 for third. Naturally, we wanted first place, but LeeRon and I and the kids surely aren't hanging our heads with third. They gave it everything they had, and that is what it is all about. And the fan support was tremendous, what more can you ask for?"

Schiley went on to say he was proud of the team. "The kids won the conference dual, district and regional championships, and went 18–2 in duals despite a terribly tough and hectic schedule with a lot of matches some weeks. Throw in the injuries and illness along the way, and you can see [we] have a special group of kids this season."

Schiley also expressed concern about the demands being put on high school wrestlers.

"The wrestling program statewide is at a point where the wrestlers are wrestling too often," Schiley told the *Reporter and Farmer*. "There were kids missing at regions due to injuries. A lot of coaches I know have at least one good kid with injury problems. I think it is because they wrestle too much."

Lesnar went into his senior year again projected to be a two-way starter in the line for the Bearcats football team, but when the Bearcats opened the season with three consecutive losses, his role changed.

The Bearcats opened with a 21–0 loss at Mobridge. The Bearcats' defense, anchored by Lesnar and expected to be the team's strength, played well—allowing only 136 yards. Lesnar had 13 tackles. The Bearcats lost their next two games—to Deuel (20–13) and Hamlin (9–0).

For the Bearcats' homecoming game against Redfield on September 15, Lesnar was switched from the line to the backfield on offense. Sparked by Lesnar, the Bearcats responded by building a 35–0 lead at halftime and went on to defeat the Pheasants, 50–0. Lesnar rushed for 113 yards and scored the Bearcats' first two touchdowns. He also had five tackles on defense.

According to the *Reporter and Farmer*, Lesnar "hadn't played running back since middle school." Lesnar's position switch was made because "the coach wanted to try a larger back in the offense."

The following week at Milbank, Lesnar scored a touchdown to help the Bearcats take an early nine-point lead, but Milbank rallied for a 14–9 victory. Lesnar rushed for 92 yards in 12 carries.

On September 29, a storm with heavy rain and lightning that arrived right before the 7:00 PM scheduled kickoff time forced the Bearcats and Aberdeen Roncalli to postpone their game until the following Monday. On October 2, the Bearcats were leading 3–2 in the third quarter when Lesnar had to leave the game because of a knee injury. Aberdeen Roncalli rallied to win the game, 8–3. Before being hurt, Lesnar had rushed for 53 yards in 13 carries and caught two passes for 28 yards.

Four days later, without Lesnar, Webster lost to Groton, 20–6. Talking about Lesnar's injury, the *Reporter and Farmer* wrote that Lesnar "may need eight weeks to recover."

The Bearcats closed out the regular season with a 13–6 loss to Clark, which was ranked No. 4 in the state 11B poll. The *Reporter and Farmer* pointed out, "A healthy Brock Lesnar would have been a big boost" to the Bearcats.

On October 19, the Bearcats season came to an end with a 14–0 playoff loss to Milbank. Josh Bohlen, whom Lesnar had pinned in a dual meet the previous school year, paced Milbank by rushing for 100 yards as the Bearcats finished with a 1–8 record. The Webster coach told the *Reporter and Farmer*, "We expected to be at least 4–4 and maybe 5–3 when the season started, but lack of consistency on offense and giving up the big play was a problem for us most of the season."

Webster High School athletic director William Sawinsky, who was an assistant football coach when Lesnar was in high school, described him as a football player, "Brock was willing to work as hard as it took to help out the team. I can remember we used him at running back, I think in his senior year, and he was a load. But, he also ran too upright and took a pounding. He eventually got hurt at running back and that kind of ended that experiment.

"I have no doubt he could have played college football, it would have had to have been at the right level, however. He was pretty raw, which is what I think the [Minnesota] Vikings kind of found out when he tried that out. It would have been interesting to see what would have happened had he chosen to go the football route out of high school, with the size and quickness he has today."

After placing second and third at the previous two state meets, the Bearcats wrestling team was expected to be a contender for the state title again in Lesnar's senior year.

Aside from Lesnar, the Bearcats had six other returning state meet qualifiers and had to replace only two seniors—Justin Gaikowski, who had qualified for the state meet, and Jason Nolte, who had missed the entire season after being injured in football.

Lesnar, who had compiled a 38–4 record as a junior, was moving up from 189 pounds to heavyweight. Lesnar had suffered a knee injury in a football game on October 2 but was ready at the start of the wrestling season.

"While one of our goals is to bring home the [state] championship trophy in February," Schiley told the *Reporter and Farmer*, "we've got two months of matches and some tough teams to face before tourney time rolls around. LeeRon and I feel that if everyone stays healthy, we stack up pretty well. If everyone stays healthy, we will have some depth this year, except at the upper weights.

"I figure we are probably among the top three Class B teams in the state this season, with [defending champion] Bon Homme, Bennett County, Stanley County, and Howard right in there. And then there are always a couple of teams who put things together by tourney time who make it even tougher for everyone else."

Before getting to the postseason, the Bearcats would have to compete with rivals Redfield, which returned its entire lineup from its conference tournament champion team of the previous season, and Milbank for the top spot in the Northeast Conference.

The knee injury didn't appear to be an issue as Lesnar opened his season with nine consecutive pins.

In the Bearcats' season-opener on November 28, Lesnar's pin (in 18 seconds) capped the Bearcats' 56–13 victory over Deuel. Eleven days later, Lesnar had four pins (each in less than 60 seconds) to help the Bearcats go 4–0 and take first place at the Watertown Tournament.

In the first match at Watertown, the Bearcats trailed the host Arrows 32–27 going into the heavyweight match. Lesnar's pin in 56 seconds lifted the Bearcats to a one-point victory. The Bearcats followed that with victories over Sioux Falls O'Gorman (49–18), Sioux Falls Washington (51–21), and Sisseton (45–15). Lesnar finished his day with a victory by pin in 25 seconds.

A week later in Groton, the Bearcats won the conference meet as Lesnar won his second conference heavyweight title. The Bearcats finished with 146.5 points—16.5 better than runner-up Redfield—as Lesnar provided 18 points with two pins and a victory by default. In the championship match, Lesnar dispatched his opponent in 15 seconds.

The Bearcats closed out 1995 by winning their own tournament on December 30. They finished with 151 points (34 more than runner-up Milbank) as Lesnar contributed two pins (in 25 seconds and 32 seconds) and a 15–0 technical fall victory in the heavyweight final.

Schiley told the *Reporter and Farmer*, "Things will be hectic from now on with an awfully busy schedule. It will be interesting to see how this tournament affects us and how much we learned."

The Bearcats started the new year with an exciting come-from-behind 33–28 victory over Redfield. The Pheasants led the match, which had seen six lead changes, 28–27 going into the heavyweight match. Lesnar's pin in 44 seconds gave the Bearcats the victory.

Schiley acknowledged to the *Reporter and Farmer*, "It's awfully nice to know that we had Brock Lesnar at heavyweight heading into the final match."

The Bearcats next defeated Madison 49–21 as Lesnar pinned his opponent in 24 seconds. Lesnar contributed two pins and a win by forfeit as the Bearcats won their next three duals easily—over DeSmet (72–0), Hamlin (63–3), and Flandreau (78–0).

On January 13, the Bearcats won the Gettysburg Tournament, but Lesnar suffered his first loss of the season. After a first-round bye, Lesnar needed just 13 seconds to pin his first opponent. But in the championship match, Doland-Conde's Jon Madsen outlasted Lesnar 4–3.

On January 20, after digging out from a winter storm that had closed school for two days and forced two duals to be postponed, the Bearcats, who were now ranked No. 3 in the state Class B poll, won the Parkston Tournament with 161 points. Philip was second with 136 points. Lesnar won by pin in his first match before defeating Scott Larson of Mobridge 7–1 in the heavyweight final.

Asked about his team's ranking in the state poll, Schiley told the *Reporter and Farmer*, "The No. 1 ranking is nice because it gives our wrestlers, team, and school a little recognition, but other than that, the ranking won't win any of the upcoming tourneys for us—the kids will have to do that, and they know that."

The Bearcats followed up with victories over Milbank (41–18), Sisseton (49–10), Groton (54–10), and Aberdeen Roncalli (68–4) as Lesnar contributed two pins, a 15–6 major decision, and a win by forfeit.

Webster closed out its regular season on January 30 by winning three duals at Clark.

The Bearcats defeated Doland-Conde 53–12, but Lesnar lost to Jon Madsen, 5–3. The Bearcats then defeated Britton 69–4, as Lesnar earned six points for his team with a victory by forfeit. In their regular-season finale, the Bearcats defeated Clark 45–17 as Lesnar closed out his regular season with a victory by pin in :27.

On February 3, the Bearcats earned their fourth consecutive district title in dominating fashion. The Bearcats advanced all 13 wrestlers to the regional tournament as they took first place with 214 points. Clark was a distant second with 147.5 points.

Lesnar won his third district title (at three different weights) by exacting a little revenge. After a first-round bye, Lesnar pinned DeSmet's Rob Cleveland in 46 seconds to advance to the championship match.

In the championship match, Lesnar outlasted Madsen, to whom he had lost by two points just four days earlier, 2–1, in two overtimes.

The Bearcats played host to the regional tournament on February 10, and for the second consecutive year, Webster and Redfield battled for the title. The Bearcats held off Redfield again for their fourth consecutive title. Webster finished with 135 points—11 more than the second-place Pheasants. A year earlier, the Bearcats had defeated the Pheasants by 11.5 points for the region title.

Lesnar won three matches to earn his first regional championship. He opened with a first-round victory by pin (in :33) and won by pin (in :45) in the second round to set up another meeting with Madsen—the third meeting in two weeks and the fourth of the season between the two wrestlers.

As they had at the district meet, Lesnar and Madsen went to a second overtime before Lesnar again prevailed, 3–2. Four years later, both Lesnar and Madsen would win an NCAA championship. In 2000, Madsen, wrestling for South Dakota State University, won the NCAA Division II heavyweight championship.

Schiley felt good about his team heading into the state meet, telling the *Reporter and Farmer*, "We're relatively healthy heading to state. [We] put a lot of pressure on the kids before the regional. Now after such a rugged schedule, we're serious and focused about going after a state title, but decided to give them a chance to unwind a little. They know what they have to do, and I know they will give it their best shot. If [we] do as well in the first two rounds as expected, how we do in the semifinals will be a key in how we finish in the team race.

"Stanley County is the most experienced, and Howard has the potential for a good tournament. Philip is the one with the most kids of about the same talent, with Bon Homme having the best chance at individual titles. We've got nine kids in, so we have as good of [a] chance as any team to win the first-place trophy. If we wrestle well, we have a shot at the title, but there are quite a few wrestlers whom I compliment with the title of 'studs' this year, and they can really mess up the team race. We'll just go out and see what happens on the mat."

Asked about Lesnar's chances at the state meet, Schiley told the newspaper, "Despite their records and being regional champs, [140-pounder] Brad [Opitz] and Brock both got tough matchups. If they advance to the semis, they'll face two-time state champions. I can't figure out how they ended up in those slots, but we're going to impress on all our wrestlers to take it one match at a time with the idea they are going to have to beat real good ones somewhere along the line anyway if they want to be state champions."

On February 16 in Aberdeen, Lesnar, who had a 30–2 record going into the state meet, had a successful first day at the state meet, winning his first two matches by fall. He opened with a pin of Tri-Valley's

Matt Baumberger in 43 seconds. In his second match in the quarterfinals, he pinned Lyman's Chad Johnson, who was 38–3 on the season, in 1:52.

But the next day in the semifinals, Lesnar was outdueled by McCook Central's Brian Van Emmerik, 4–1. Lesnar came back to defeat Scott Larson of Mobridge 4–1 in the wrestlebacks to advance to the third-place match.

In the third-place match, Lesnar pinned Johnson, whom he had also pinned in the quarterfinals the day before, in 3:46. Van Emmerik, who would go on to play college football for the University of Wyoming, went on to win his third consecutive state title and was named the MVP of the meet.

The Bearcats finished second in the team standings with 88.5 points. Howard won its first state title with 102.5 points.

"One more win along the way and maybe a loss on the other side and we could have been state champions," Schiley told the *Reporter and Farmer*. "That's how close it was."

In its season recap, the *Reporter and Farmer* mentioned the welcome-home program for the Bearcats. Webster Superintendent Arnie Anderson told the group, "I know you are disappointed you didn't win state, but that is one thing about athletics, they help you learn to handle disappointment. There will always be stumbling blocks in life, but you know how to come back from disappointments and can bounce back there, too."

Another speaker at the program was former Webster wrestler Mike Wiley, who had refereed at the state meet.

Wiley, who had won three state titles—in 1979 and 1980 at 98 pounds and in 1982 at 112 pounds—told the group, "You can be proud of all the things you overcame this season. You were faced with injuries but overcame them. You beat Watertown for the first time in many years, and the Arrows were State A runners-up. You beat Redfield and picked up a lot of wins during the season with pins or by picking up points when you were behind. This was just your first match in life."

The second-place finish at the state meet capped an outstanding four seasons for the Bearcats. The Bearcats had gone 25–0 in dual meets, making them 76–6 in dual meets over the last four seasons. The Bearcats had won 26 tournaments in the last four seasons and had compiled a 1,904–501 won-lost record (a .792 winning percentage) in individual matches.

The last four seasons were part of a nine-year period that saw the Bearcats go 156–31–1 in dual meets and win 34 of the 45 tournaments they entered. In that period, Webster wrestlers had won 3,000 of 4,000 individual matches (a .750 winning percentage).

As his high school career came to an end, Lesnar, who could dead lift 600 pounds as a senior, was uncertain about his future. He hadn't been recruited as a wrestler. Nearby Northern State University, an NCAA Division II school located in Aberdeen about 45 miles west of Webster, offered Lesnar, who had played three of years of varsity football as an offensive lineman, a football scholarship. But Mike Wiley, who had spoken to the team after the state meet, would have something to say about Lesnar's future.

DAVE MADSEN

The first time Dave Madsen wrestled Brock Lesnar was when Madsen was 10 years old. "It was at a state AAU tournament," Madsen said. "I got creamed."

Despite that, the two went on to be friends. "I lived about 45 minutes from Webster," said Madsen, who went to school in Doland, South Dakota. "We were good friends. We would see each other often. At dual meets. At tournaments."

Madsen and Lesnar wrestled each other twice in high school. As a junior, Lesnar defeated Madsen 8–2 for the 189-pound title at the

Gettysburg Tournament, and he defeated Madsen 4–2 for the 189-pound title at the Britton Tournament. But Madsen dropped down a weight, and they didn't meet again that season.

"The thing I remember the most about wrestling Brock was his strength. He could grab your wrists and control you."

In Lesnar's senior year, he wrestled Madsen's younger brother, Jon, four times. Jon Madsen won the first two matches—Lesnar lost only one other match during his senior season—but Lesnar won the next two in overtime.

"They were incredible matches," Dave Madsen said. "For a small town, there were 2,000 people in the gym. One side of the gym was yelling for Brock, and the other was yelling 'Go Mad Dog' for Jon. They were intense matches, snot flying. I don't think there were any takedowns. That's how Brock won, he just ended up riding out Jon. I think wrestling Jon helped Brock develop his skills. He changed his stance."

After beating Jon Madsen in the district and regional finals, Lesnar went on to finish third at the South Dakota Class B state meet.

"Brock's senior year, any one of four [heavyweights] could have been a state champ," Dave Madsen said. "He very easily could have been a state champ. I went into the locker room after his final at the state meet. He was tore up. Not winning a state title lit a fire for him. I remember staying at his house, and he would have a dozen eggs for breakfast for the protein. His competitiveness was second to none."

After high school, Lesnar passed up an offer to play football for Northern State (in Aberdeen, South Dakota) to enroll at Bismarck State College.

"He tried to get me to go up there with him," said Dave Madsen, who chose to go to Huron where he wrestled for one year and played football for three years.

Dave Madsen and Lesnar wrestled again at an open tournament in 1998, with Lesnar winning.

Dave Madsen is currently a teacher and wrestling coach at Simi Valley (California) High School. After high school, Jon Madsen attended South Dakota State University. In 2000, the same year that Lesnar won the NCAA Division I heavyweight title, Jon Madsen won the NCAA Division II heavyweight title. After his college career, where he was a two-time All-America selection, Jon Madsen started training in mixed martial arts. In early 2010, Madsen was a UFC fighter with a 5–0 record.

BOB HIRSCH

By the time he was a freshman, Brock Lesnar was developing into a good high school wrestler.

Bob Hirsch, the coach of a rival South Dakota wrestling team during Lesnar's high school career, said, "I remember when he was a freshman, we [Milbank] had a senior who was pretty good and was fourth in the state. The first time they wrestled, our guy won 13–7. The next time they wrestled, our guy won 12–8. The last time they wrestled that season was at the conference meet, and our guy won 11–10. But after the match he said, 'I don't want to wrestle that guy again.' At that point, I think Brock had started his metamorphoses."

Hirsch, who coached Milbank to a first- or second-place finish at the South Dakota State Class B meet four times between 1990 and 1995, had witnessed Lesnar take his lumps the previous two years as a seventh and eighth grader on the Webster varsity.

"As a coach, you have to stay positive with a young wrestler," said Hirsch, a Vermillion, South Dakota, high school product who won a South Dakota state title and was an All-American in college for Northern State. "You have to help him realize his potential. Us wrestling coaches have an old saying, 'Hard work breeds success.' You have to have a march forward, drive on attitude. Most kids in South Dakota do. Brock certainly did."

Lesnar continued to develop as a high school wrestler. As a junior, he helped Webster defeat Milbank in a dual meet for the first time in more than 20 years. Lesnar's pin at heavyweight completed the 32–24 victory.

"I remember it was a rescheduled match we held at the Milbank Middle School," Hirsch said. "We knew it would be a real tough match. Their kids were building a tough program. It was pretty intense. We had to juggle our lineup because one of our wrestlers didn't wrestle because his father passed away the morning of the meet. I didn't realize it was Webster's first win over us until a couple of days later. I'm sure the Webster people realized it right away."

Hirsch also saw Lesnar compete on the football field. "He was brutal, he was a monster," Hirsch said. "There weren't a lot of kids like him around. He really had a presence on the football field."

After Lesnar finished high school, he went on to wrestle at Bismarck (North Dakota) State College. Hirsch was able to follow Lesnar's development there as well.

"It was kind of neat," said Hirsch, who is now a teacher and wrestling coach at Watertown (South Dakota) High School. "In addition to coaching, I officiate college wrestling. And when Brock was at Bismarck, I officiated at the regional and national [JC] tournament at Bismarck. It was really eye-popping for me to see what a wrestler that thin kid from Webster had turned into.

"I remember a conversation I had with his JUCO coach. He told me Brock was unusual 'Because most kids you've got to pull them into the weight room. With Brock, you've got to pull him out.' He was a workout maniac."

Hirsch was also in attendance at the 1999 and 2000 NCAA Division I wrestling championships when Lesnar wrestled Cal State Bakersfield's Stephen Neal (in 1999) and Iowa's Wes Hand (in 2000) for the heavyweight title.

"He's just a good guy," Hirsch said, "a class act. Very personable. Whenever we bump into each other, he says, 'Hi coach.' Last summer

[2009], I was at a tournament in Fargo [North Dakota] and we bumped into each other at a restaurant. We stood and talked for 20 minutes. People were coming up to take his picture with their cell phones, and he told me to get in the pictures."

CHAPTER 3

BECOMING A COLLEGE WRESTLER

Falling short of a state title in high school motivated Lesnar. On the *Here Comes the Pain* DVD, he said, "Growing up and going through school, some of my goals were to be a state champion, I didn't succeed in those, that's what drove myself to get bigger, stronger, faster, quicker on the mat. I wanted to be a college wrestler, and I do believe if I would have won a state title, I wouldn't even be sitting here talking to you today probably because I had some unfinished business to do. I knew that in my heart."

In May 2009, Lesnar told *Maxim* magazine, "I was always fascinated by strength. Arnold [Schwarzenegger] was an idol of mine. I thought I was going to be a farmer."

Lesnar went on to say in the magazine interview, that a brief stint in the National Guard led to an epiphany. "I wanted to go to school. I wanted to wrestle. I wanted to be something."

The Bismarck State wrestling staff already had a heavyweight it was counting on heading into the 1996–97 school year. But Mike Wiley, who had gone from Webster High School to become a two-time All-America for Bismarck State in the mid-1980s, convinced the wrestling staff to take a look at a wrestler from his hometown. Wiley also convinced that wrestler to consider Bismarck.

Lesnar told the *Bismarck Tribune* in June 2005 that he had originally planned to work for a year after high school while considering his academic future, but "one guy from my hometown [Wiley] called Ed [Bismarck athletic director Kringstad] and told him about me in late July or early August. Then things fell into place. I packed my bags up and in a couple of weeks I was off to school. Before I knew it, I'm in Bismarck. I've got an old Monte Carlo with snow tires on the back, it's September, and I've got maybe $100 to my name, and I'm living in Ed Kringstad's basement. Life brings you weird things. A lot of schools wanted me to play football for them, but my heart has always been in wrestling. I've been wrestling since I was in kindergarten."

Kringstad told the *Bismarck Tribune*, "[Wiley] said he thinks [Lesnar] has a lot of potential. Wiley, I knew, knows wrestling, so I just went with that. This kid showed up, and he was awesome."

Lesnar, who weighed 210 pounds when he got to Bismarck, breezed through his first college wrestling regular season and took a 14–2 record into the NJCAA North Central Regional in Rochester, Minnesota. At the regional, Lesnar and seven of his Mystics teammates qualified for the NJCAA National meet. Another teammate received a berth in the national meet when a wrestler pulled out. According to co-coach Bruce Basaraba, the nine Bismarck qualifiers for the national meet was likely a school record.

Previewing the national meet, Basaraba told the *Bismarck Tribune*, "If he [Lesnar] wrestles well, he has a really good chance of making the finals."

Lesnar took an 18–2 record into the national meet, which was being held in Bismarck for the eighth consecutive year. The tournament, which had 248 competitors, began on Friday, February 28.

The first round started on a positive note for the Mystics, as 118-pound Rob Barchenger won his first-round match 6–3. But after Barchenger's victory, the Mystics lost seven consecutive first-round matches. Lesnar stopped that streak with his 7–0 first-round victory over Tim Ellis of Harper (Illinois) College.

In the second round, Lesnar got a takedown with 14 seconds remaining in the third period to rally for a 3–2 victory over Gordon Campbell of Muskegon, Michigan.

But in the quarterfinals, Lesnar was outlasted by Damion Martindale of Clackamas (Oregon) 5–4. Martindale held on for the victory when he avoided a takedown by Lesnar with 10 seconds remaining.

"That was a tough one to swallow," Basaraba told the *Bismarck Tribune*.

Lesnar had fallen behind 4–1 early in the match.

"He got tossed on a four-point move and was down 4–1 right away," Basaraba told the *Bismarck Tribune*.

Despite the loss, Lesnar could still finish as high as third place by winning four consecutive consolation matches. But he fell just short of that, going 3–1 to take fifth place. In the fifth-place match, he pinned Lincoln's Mike Russow in 2:57.

The fifth-place finish was disappointing for Lesnar, who had compiled a respectable 23–5 record during his freshman season.

"He thought he had a chance of winning the title," Basaraba said. "That one really motivated him."

Over the summer, Lesnar worked out and added 20 pounds of muscle.

"He succeeded by his work ethic," Basaraba said. "Just three weeks ago [in the fall of 2009], I looked at a picture of him from his first year at Bismarck. He looked like a butterball. He was in shape but had a little baby fat. In the next year's picture, he was more defined. He really matured while he was at Bismarck."

Lesnar opened his sophomore season by going undefeated in open tournaments at North Dakota State, South Dakota State, Augsburg (in Minneapolis), and the University of Minnesota–Morris.

On January 21, 1998, a dual meet against the University of Mary (an NAIA school located in Bismarck), gave Lesnar the opportunity to wrestle a familiar opponent—Scott Owens. Owens, the top-ranked heavyweight in the NAIA, and Lesnar had met once the previous season (Owens won 1–0) and twice already in the 1997–98 season.

In addition to those two matches—won by Lesnar by pin and a 5–1 decision—the two frequently worked out together.

"We've wrestled quite a lot," Lesnar told the *Bismarck Tribune*. "I go out and practice with him quite often. I try to see him twice a week, so we've become good friends off the mat."

Lesnar, who brought a 21–0 record into the dual meet, pinned Owens in 3:07. Mary won the dual though, 32–12.

After the match, Lesnar told the *Bismarck Tribune* he was focused on one thing.

"I'm going to win it. I'm going to be a national champion this year," Lesnar said. "I've been wrestling too long and working too hard to let this one go."

Three days after the dual with Mary, Lesnar won the heavyweight title at the Marauder Invitational, hosted by Mary. Lesnar defeated Augsburg's Jose Pena 9–0 in the heavyweight championship match.

As the Mystics prepared to play host to the NJCAA national meet again, school officials announced it was going to drop wrestling as an intercollegiate sport at the end of the season. The school had first fielded a wrestling team in 1961.

Ironically, the person making the announcement was Athletic Director Ed Kringstad, who had coached the wrestling team for 24 seasons. Kringstad told the *Bismarck Tribune* that the decision to drop the sport was "based only in part on economics. We're running around the country too much. We only had one home dual. We used to have five or six home duals. It's an economic factor in that we have to travel so far and can't get home gates, but the major factor was that we had to travel so much. These kids came here to go to school."

Kringstad added that the timing of the decision made sense. "We've got all sophomores except for one kid, so if we're going to drop it, the time to do it is now."

Going into the national meet, the hope was that the program would go out in style with a victory by Lesnar in the heavyweight championship match—the final match of the NJCAA meet and in school history.

Lesnar, who had started his sophomore season ranked No. 3 at heavyweight in the NJCAA preseason poll, had moved up to No. 1 in the rankings with a 29–0 record.

Bismarck State co-coach Robert Finneseth described Lesnar's season to the *Bismarck Tribune* for its preview of the national meet.

"He's really matured," Finneseth said. "I think he's been looking forward to the big matches. It's been awhile since he was pushed. He's looking forward to the type of matches you see in the Bison Open [hosted by North Dakota State] and the South Dakota State tournament. I wasn't sure how he would do [at the regional tournament in Willmar, Minnesota], but he really cranked it up. So I think he's ready to go."

Lesnar, who was bidding to become Bismarck State's 11th—and final—NJCAA champion, opened his title bid with two pins to advance to the semifinals. After a first-round bye, he pinned John Cox of Corning (New York) in 24 seconds. In the quarterfinals, he pinned Matt Carter of Northwest Wyoming in 1:37. Carter had advanced to the quarterfinals by pinning his first two opponents.

In the semifinals, he wrestled Clackamas (Oregon) sophomore Leo Sandoval, who was 26–14 on the season and had won three matches to reach the semifinals. Lesnar defeated Sandoval 3–1 to advance.

In the championship match, Lesnar faced a nemesis from his freshman year—Dave Anderton of Ricks, Idaho. Anderton had followed a similar path to the finals. After a first-round bye, he won his first two matches by pin before winning 7–1 in the semifinals.

Anderton had defeated Lesnar twice the previous season—by a 3–2 decision and a pin.

"Those are the kind of things that just burn in you," Lesnar told the *Bismarck Tribune*.

Lesnar and Anderton dazzled the crowd with a wide-open match.

Midway through the first period, Lesnar had a 5–0 lead after locking up Anderton in a cradle. But Anderton recovered in the second period, and after taking down Lesnar late in the period, the match was tied 6–6. After the two traded reversals, the match was tied 8–8 going into the final period.

Anderton started the third period in the down position and finally broke free with 15 seconds remaining for an escape and a 9–8 lead. But Lesnar immediately got a takedown for a 10–9 lead. Lesnar held on for the remaining 13 seconds, and riding time gave him an additional point for an 11–9 victory.

"It could probably have gone either way," Lesnar told the *Bismarck Tribune*. "I wanted it more. I know I did. I got a little anxious and let him back in it. In the long run, this match will help me tremendously. I'll be more patient."

Anderton told the *Bismarck Tribune* he was aware Lesnar liked to go for the cradle.

"I know he had the cradle," Anderton said. "But this year he's got a lot more strength."

Lesnar told the newspaper, "I've been using it since I was little. I'm strong and have long arms, so I can get it in."

Lesnar had lived up to the potential Basaraba and Wiley thought he had.

"Did he have potential when he came to Bismarck? Oh yes," Basaraba said. "Just by the way all he wanted to do was sit in a room and learn stuff. His first year, he wrestled a big guy. Brock did a double-leg takedown. We have a picture of it; both guys are 6 inches off the ground. That's the kind of force he had. If we wanted guys to stay late and learn something new, he always would stick around. Once he put his mind to something, he did it.

"To be successful, you just have to have the mental toughness to go into the weight room every day. It's like running every morning. You get up and you're stiff or something, so you decide not to run that day. He never took a day off. I think after awhile, he just got to thinking of it as a way of life. Kind of, 'This is what I do.' Some days in the wrestling room at the end of practice, we would do [extra] conditioning. Everybody would be exhausted, but Brock still had energy [afterwards] to go lift."

In June 2005, Lesnar was elected to the Bismarck State College Hall of Fame.

"It's pretty awesome that I'm getting inducted, getting to hang a piece of me in here, because this [place] is a piece of me," Lesnar told the *Bismarck Tribune* at the induction ceremony. "When I came here today, and I'm sitting and talking in front of the BSC Foundation for lunch, I got choked up. This is where it all started. I remember those people [who] helped me out. I remember Ed Kringstad, [athletic secretary] Dee [Bertsch], the Katzes—everybody [who] was there to give me a helping hand or a kick in the rear."

Lesnar went on to admit to the newspaper that he was "a little bitter about the wrestling program not being here. I'm a little chapped about that. As I walk around the facility and I see back when they dropped the program. It was a money issue. Now it's five years or six years later, and I'm walking around this facility, and there's all these new buildings going up, and I'm seeing this new cafeteria and all these other things. Well, where's the new wrestling room? That's kind of hard for me to swallow."

But any hard feelings didn't stop Lesnar from helping with some fund-raising for the school.

"I want to give these kids who are coming out of high school—like me—I just wanted them to feel special at a small school," Lesnar told the newspaper. "That's why I'm here, to give back, and let the people know that I appreciated everything they've done, and I want to give these other kids opportunities."

Lesnar went on to recall his first year in Bismarck for the newspaper:

"For me, the one thing that sticks out is that I didn't know what I was getting myself into," Lesnar said. "I remember just struggling. I wasn't the greatest wrestler out of high school, and I was going against and meeting guys [who] were better than me. I was wrestling with them and I just kept hammering away. Not only on the wrestling mat, but in the classroom as well. Every day was a battle and something new.

"My national [junior college] championship was, for me, a weight lifted off my shoulder. And then it was like, 'No, that wasn't good enough. I want some more, and let's see where we could go with it.'"

CHAPTER 4

NCAA CHAMPION

University of Minnesota wrestling coach J Robinson built a successful program with his ability to recruit.

Ten times in his first 23 seasons as the Gophers coach, Robinson and his staff brought in a recruiting class that was ranked No. 1 in the nation by recruiting experts. That recruiting paid off in three NCAA titles and a top-three finish at the NCAA meet nine times in a 12-year span.

Recruiting can be hard work and time consuming. And sometimes it can just be serendipitous.

On November 15, 1997, the Gophers opened their 1997–98 season at the Bison Open, hosted by North Dakota State in Fargo, North Dakota. Among the 200 or so wrestlers competing at the invitational was Bismarck State Junior College sophomore Brock Lesnar.

Lesnar was the only non-University of Minnesota wrestler to win a championship at the meet.

"Our heavyweight, Shelton Benjamin, got beat in the semis, and he got beat by a kid from Nebraska, who then ended up wrestling this guy from Bismarck Junior College in the finals and that was Brock," Robinson said. "And that's the first time that we ever saw him or had anything to do with him. So Brock beat the kid pretty easily from Nebraska, so basically I just went up right after the tournament was over and introduced myself.

"I asked him if he was looking to wrestle in college, and he said yes. I asked him if he'd be interested in coming down on a visit, and he said yes. So we brought him in on Sunday, he was here on Sunday and Monday. He went home and signed on Tuesday. We never really heard about him; we just kind of stumbled on him more than anything else. And then once we saw him wrestle, then it just became, it became more of a deal of…you know…here's this guy, a lot of people don't know about, and we have to make sure we get him before anybody finds out he's out there."

On November 20, five days after being spotted by the Gophers coaching staff, Lesnar was one of six—another recruiting class that would be ranked No. 1 in the nation—to sign letters of intent to wrestle for the Gophers.

"In the South Dakota State Open and that tournament [the Bison Open]," Lesnar told the *Bismarck Tribune*, "I had a lot of coaches talking to me, and I wanted to find a home so I could stop dealing with the phone calls and the questions."

On the *Here Comes the Pain* DVD, Lesnar said, "That's when a lot of the bigger Division I schools were interested in me. Number one I had a great physique, I was a great athlete, and I was in great condition, and I could wrestle. There's not very many heavyweights out there [who] are built like me, [who] can go like me. So, I was a hot commodity for a couple of weeks before I decided where I was going to wrestle."

In the fall of 1998, Lesnar enrolled at the University of Minnesota. But as a transfer, he didn't become eligible until the second semester. While waiting to become eligible, Lesnar worked out with the team and wrestled unattached in the Bison Open. Lesnar won the heavyweight title—pinning Gophers teammate Brent Boeshans—as the Gophers won all 10 weight divisions at the Bison Open for the first time. Lesnar became eligible for the Gophers on January 4 after completing some class work from Bismarck.

The Gophers, who had finished third at the NCAA Championships in 1997 and second in 1998, were ranked No. 2 in the nation and were expected to be a top contender for the NCAA title in 1999.

"I want to put the icing on the cake," Lesnar told the *Minneapolis Star Tribune*. "I can't do much more. They have such a great team already, just maybe give that little extra edge."

On January 9, Lesnar wrestled in the Great Plains Open in Lincoln, Nebraska, winning three matches before losing to Iowa State's Trent Hynek 5–3 in the championship match.

A week later, Lesnar shed his unknown label.

On January 16–17, the Gophers, whose second-place finish at the NCAA meet the previous year was the best finish in school history, and were ranked No. 2 in the NCAA preseason poll, and the other top college wrestling programs gathered in Iowa City, Iowa, for the Cliff Kean/NWCA National Duals. Lesnar would made quite an impression as he pinned all four of his opponents in the two-day meet—Augsburg's Ben Bauer (0:50), Central Michigan's Jack Leffler (1:52), Iowa's Wes Hand (2:36), and Oklahoma State's Todd Munson (3:54).

Lesnar's victory over Hand, who was ranked No. 2 in the *Amateur Wrestling News* national heavyweight rankings, clinched the Gophers' 21–14 victory over Iowa—just the second time in school history the Gophers had beaten the Hawkeyes in Iowa City. The first time had been the previous season, when the Gophers won 18–17 in the National Duals.

Lesnar's performance earned him the Big Ten Wrestler of the Week award and vaulted him from No. 9 to No. 2 in the national heavyweight rankings.

"He'll win a lot of matches when people are warming up across the mat from him," Robinson told the *Minneapolis Star Tribune*. "I don't think there's anybody [who's] bigger. I've been in this 25 years, and I've never seen a guy built as big and strong and powerful as he is."

On January 22, the Gophers opened the Big Ten dual-meet portion of their schedule with a 23–17 victory over Michigan in Minneapolis. The dual was tied going into the heavyweight match before Lesnar pinned the Wolverines' Matt Brink in 2:20.

The next night the Gophers easily handled Michigan State 27–10, as Lesnar contributed an 11–3 victory over the Spartans' Matt Lamb.

The following weekend, the Gophers made a return trip to Iowa. Lesnar provided a crucial three team points to the Gophers' 19–17 victory—their third consecutive victory over the Hawkeyes in Iowa City—with a 6–0 victory over Wes Hand.

The Gophers and Lesnar cruised through the remainder of the regular season unbeaten. Lesnar won six matches—two by pin—to improve to 16–1 with six pins.

The Gophers, led by Lesnar, who was the No. 1 seed at heavyweight, went into the Big Ten Championships in Ann Arbor, Michigan, looking for their first conference title in 50 years.

Lesnar went 4–0 and defeated Karl Roesler of Illinois 7–0 in the heavyweight championship match to lead the Gophers to the team title with 139 points—18 more than runner-up Iowa. The Gophers' title ended Iowa's streak of 25 consecutive conference championships.

Less than two weeks later, at the NCAA meet, the Gophers and Iowa had another showdown.

At the NCAA meet, the Hawkeyes were wrestling for their fifth consecutive—and eighth in nine years—NCAA title. The Gophers, who finished 13 points behind the Hawkeyes at the NCAA meet the previous season, were hoping that they could ride their regular-season and conference-meet success against Iowa to earn their first NCAA title.

The three-day meet, hosted by Penn State University, wasn't decided until the final match.

In the next-to-last match of the meet, the Gophers pulled within two points of first-place Iowa in the overall team standings after the Gophers' Tim Hartung defeated Iowa's Lee Fullhart in the 197-pound championship match. Hartung's victory meant that if Lesnar defeated Cal State Bakersfield's Stephen Neal, the defending NCAA champion, in the heavyweight championship match, the Gophers would win the title.

But Lesnar, who had cruised through his first four matches of the NCAA meet—winning 12–2, by pin in 22 seconds, 4–0 and 10–2—came up short as Neal pulled out a 3–2 victory for his second NCAA title. A first-period takedown was the difference for Neal, who capped his second consecutive unbeaten season with his 83rd consecutive victory.

Lesnar told the *Minneapolis Star Tribune*, "He's a good athlete. I gave all I had, wrestled 110 percent, but it didn't happen out there. It wasn't just me, there were a lot of us. I knew if I won, we won, but it could've come down to any one of us—that's what the team aspect of it all is."

It was the first time in 24 years that the NCAA Division I team wrestling champion wasn't determined until the final match of the meet. Iowa won the title with 100.5 points, two points more than the Gophers.

Later in 1999, Neal went on to become the U.S. Freestyle champion, winning the Pan American Games and the world championship. Neal then went on to a career in the National Football League.

"I don't know if anyone has ever pinned it [not winning the NCAA title] on Brock," Robinson recalled in an interview in 2009. "I don't remember anybody saying that. I remember most of the guys on the team think more along the lines that 'If I had done this, if I had done that,' you know?

"I mean, there's lots of things that happened in that tournament that could have tipped the scales for us. There were guys from Iowa that got calls that were, you know, maybe questionable calls. There was Chad Kraft, who lost the flip of a coin in the overtime, in overtime in the semis, if he had won the flip and goes down and we win, we win the tournament. The reality comes down to Michael Jordan's got the ball and he's got the last shot, that's, you know, it's not fair, but you know that's the way people look at it. You know [former Gophers heavyweight] Cole Konrad is an example. Someone told me, that 17 times during his career it came down to him."

Lesnar went into the 1999–2000 pictured on the cover of the Gophers media guide and ranked No. 1 in the heavyweight preseason rankings.

"He is a specimen, there is no doubt about it," Robinson said in the Gophers' season outlook. "A lot of people came to our meets last year just to see what he looks like. I guess he has become some kind of phenomenon."

Lesnar's senior season got off to a slow start because of illness and minor injuries, but he eventually lived up to his preseason billing.

On November 13, 1999, the Gophers and Lesnar opened their season, as usual, at the Bison Open. Lesnar won his first two matches by pin before beating teammate Garrett Lowney 3–2 for the heavyweight championship.

Lesnar won his next three matches—by pin, major decision, and forfeit—as the Gophers won dual meets from North Dakota State, St. Cloud State, and Hofstra. Lesnar wrestled just two matches in December—winning by major decision and pin to improve to 8–0.

Heading into a dual meet with No. 8 Nebraska on January 7, Robinson thought his unbeaten (5–0) and No. 4-ranked Gophers were complacent. At practice two days before the match, Robinson urged his team to start showing more intensity. Lesnar and his teammates responded.

The match opened at 197 pounds with a Cornhuskers victory. Up next was the heavyweight match, and Lesnar overpowered his opponent. Lesnar had his opponent on his back immediately and went on to earn a pin in 39 seconds. The six points gave the Gophers a spark as they won three of the next four matches and went on to defeat the Cornhuskers 29–13.

"I was just excited to get back on the mat," Lesnar told the *Minneapolis Star Tribune*. "Any time you get some momentum going, it really helps the team. It got the ball rolling."

Two days later, Lesnar lifted the Gophers to a 19–15 victory over No. 3 Oklahoma State in Stillwater, Oklahoma. The host Cowboys led 15–13 going into the final match, but Lesnar pinned the Cowboys' Dave Anderton—whom he had defeated in the NJCAA heavyweight championship match two years earlier—in 3:48 to give the Gophers the victory. The loss ended the Cowboys' 73-match unbeaten streak, which dated to 1996.

Robinson, who graduated from Oklahoma State, was pleased with his team.

"This was really a great win for our whole team," Robinson told the *Minneapolis Star Tribune*. "It reinforced everything that we believe in. From Friday [Nebraska] to Sunday [Oklahoma State], this team changed their whole attitude and really made a statement with their wrestling, whether they were going to win or lose."

The following weekend, the Gophers opened their Big Ten schedule on the road with dual-meet victories at Penn State and Ohio State. Lesnar defeated Penn State's Mark Janus 10–6 and pinned Ohio State's Tony Sylvester in 51 seconds.

On January 22, the Gophers returned to Penn State for the National Duals. The Gophers (9–0), who were ranked No. 3 in the nation, were the No. 2 seed behind Iowa State for the two-day, 16-team meet.

The Gophers easily dispatched Montana State–Northern as Lesnar won by pin in 31 seconds and defeated Seth Charles of Cornell to set up a rematch with Oklahoma State in the semifinals.

Lesnar again rescued the Gophers. The Gophers trailed 15–12 going into the match, but Lesnar defeated Anderton 13–3 to provide the Gophers four points and a 16–15 victory. The victory put the Gophers to the championship match against Iowa State, which was ranked No. 2.

Iowa State held on for a 17–16 victory over the Gophers—the Gophers' first loss of the season, which ended a school-record 23-match winning streak.

The Cyclones led 17–12 going into the heavyweight match. A pin by Lesnar would again lift the Gophers to the victory. But Lesnar wasn't able to pin the Cyclones' Mark Knauer, winning instead by major decision 11–3.

The Gophers returned home for dual-meet victories over Wisconsin and Indiana. In the victory over Wisconsin—Robinson's 200th as a head coach—Lesnar started out the match with a pin. Against Indiana, Lesnar won 7–1.

On February 5, the Gophers defeated Illinois 30–6. Lesnar pinned the Illini's Karl Roesler in a match that amazed former Gophers heavyweight and current assistant coach Billy Pierce.

Pierce, who won a Big Ten title and 142 matches (51 by pin) and was a three-time All-America selection during his college career, told the *Minneapolis Star Tribune*:

"Brock put the Illinois heavyweight in a cradle I couldn't believe. The Illini guy, Karl Roesler, is a good heavyweight—rated sixth or seventh in the country. Brock got him in the cradle and had Roesler's right knee on the mat, behind his ear. You don't see that with heavyweights. The guy was screaming. The ref finally stopped the match. I thought he had pulled a hamstring or something. It turned out the cradle chipped a bone in the Illinois kid's hip.

"I've seen him walk onto the mat, and you watch the opponent and you see the fear in their eyes. He's so top heavy that he's intimidating. Some of the duals I've seen, the guys are beaten before the dual even starts. Even some of the top-ranked guys, they're beaten before they even go out there."

On February 7, Lesnar remained unbeaten with a tough 5–4 decision over Penn's Bandele Adeniyi-Bada at the NWCA All-Star Classic.

The Gophers won their next three dual meets over Michigan, Michigan State, and Northwestern as Lesnar recorded two more pins.

In the final week of the regular season, a story in the *Minneapolis Star Tribune* talked about Lesnar's rising profile in the Twin Cities. The story mentioned Lesnar's weekly appearance on a Twin Cities radio station. His first appearance on KFAN generated so much positive feedback that he was made a regular. The show, "Minnesota Wrestling Weekly," had become a success on a local sports cable outlet mainly because of Lesnar. Earlier in the month, prior to the Wisconsin and Indiana meets, the Gophers athletic department handed out posters of Lesnar to the first 500 fans. The poster, titled "Brockfast of Champions," featured a growth chart with Lesnar's neck and biceps measurements.

"A guy like him—he draws in a different kind of fan," Gophers assistant coach Marty Morgan was quoted in the story. "Our society has always been draw to big people. Pretty soon your average person on the street knows who Brock Lesnar is when you wouldn't maybe know who some of our All-Americans were."

In the article, Lesnar was asked about his future. He responded, "I think about wrestling all the time. If it was gone, I don't know what I would think about. Right now I don't know what I want to do. The only vision I have is to be happy and comfortable."

The No. 2 Gophers closed out the regular season with a showdown against top-ranked Iowa. With a crowd of 13,128 on hand in Williams Arena—the largest crowd, at the time, to see a college wrestling dual meet on campus—the Hawkeyes, who had lost three of their previous four duals to the Gophers, pulled out a 20–13 victory.

The match started at 141 pounds, and going into the heavyweight match between the 265-pound Lesnar and the 6'1", 250-pound Wes Hand, the Gophers had a 13–10 lead. Hand, who had lost to Lesnar twice in the previous season (by pin in 2:36 and by a 6–0 decision), built a 4–0 lead and then held on for a 5–3 victory—Lesnar's first loss of the season in 23 matches. After taking the four-point lead, Hand became conservative so that Lesnar couldn't use his size to get underneath him.

"It's to be expected. Guys are sitting back on me this year," Lesnar told the *Minneapolis Star Tribune*. "It's real smart on their part. Hand wrestled a great match, and he did what he had to do."

"I think in that match, Brock was a little tense, and there again, there was a little pressure involved, he was tentative about how he wrestled," Robinson said in a later interview. "Hand kind of caught him by surprise, you know, and then it was a catch-up game. He might have been a little overly aggressive, and it ended up hurting him."

Lesnar told the *Minneapolis Star Tribune* that the Gophers would learn from their mistakes against Iowa as they prepared for the postseason.

"Better to lose now than then," Lesnar said.

In two weeks, Hand and Lesnar would meet again at the Big Ten Championships. The victory over Lesnar earned Hand the top seed at heavyweight for the conference meet. Lesnar, the defending Big Ten champion, was the No. 2 seed.

On March 4, Lesnar won his first two matches (by pin in 2:31 and by an 8–1 decision) to earn a spot in the semifinals against John Lockhart of Illinois. Lesnar outlasted Lockhart 2–1 to earn a rematch with Hand.

In the finals, Lesnar avenged his only loss by outlasting Hand 2–1. Despite Hand's loss, the Hawkeyes had four champions and edged the Gophers by seven points for their 26th Big Ten Conference title in 27 seasons.

"I wait my whole life for this stuff, Big Tens and NCAAs," Lesnar told the *Minneapolis Star Tribune*. "This has been a hard year, and coming off my loss from Hand, it was good to win this match. A 'W' is a 'W.'"

Robinson told the newspaper, "This is not the end of our season. The NCAAs are the most important, and that is what we want the most. We will go back and think about what we did right and what we did wrong and go from there."

Two weeks later at the NCAA Championships in St. Louis, Lesnar opened his title bid with a 4–2 victory in the first round over Boise State's Bart Johnson. He followed up that victory with pins over Lehigh's Shawn Laughlin (in 2:18) and Ohio's Tim Courtad (in 4:04) to advance to the semifinals.

In the semifinals, Lesnar wrestled Adeniyi-Bada, whom he had defeated 5–4 a month earlier. This time, Lesnar pinned Adeniyi-Bada in the third period to advance to the championship match against Hand.

In a defensive struggle, Lesnar led 1–0 after two periods. Despite trailing, Hand elected to start the third period in the up position. Lesnar quickly escaped to take a 2–0 lead. But late in the period, Lesnar was called for stalling twice, and Hand was awarded points to tie the match 2–2.

After a scoreless first overtime, Lesnar won the coin flip before the second overtime. Lesnar escaped with 9 seconds remaining for a 3–2 victory. Lesnar became the first Gophers heavyweight to win an NCAA championship in 51 years.

"I didn't want it to come down to double overtime," Lesnar told the *Minneapolis Star Tribune*, "but I'll take it. I'm excited."

Lesnar's parents and high school coach were in attendance and recalled the match on the *Here Comes the Pain* DVD.

"Well, I'll tell you that championship match was probably harder on his mother and I," Richard Lesnar said. "My wife said, 'You're going to go into cardiac arrest or something.' I guess I was all white and just yelling and screaming."

Stephanie Lesnar said, "They were so darn close throughout the whole match, and I mean his opponent was out to get him because Brock had done him in several times."

Schiley said, "We knew it was going to be a big tough match, and it got down to the double overtime."

Justin Gaikowski, a friend of Brock's, said, "That was the only thing that mattered to him, money didn't matter to him, nothing, just that match."

Brock Lesnar commented, "When my hand was raised, winning that NCAA title, it was like a big weight was lifted off of me, and I had accomplished everything. I looked up at my mom and dad in the stands and I looked at my high school wrestling coach who was there watching me, and I just couldn't remember that feeling of just like, 'Man, I did it. I finally did it.'"

Stephanie Lesnar summed up Brock's victory. "It was a dream come true."

The victory gave Lesnar a 31–1 record (with 15 pins) for the season. In two years with the Gophers, Lesnar was 55–3 with 23 pins. He had become the first Minnesota heavyweight to win an NCAA championship since Verne Gagne in 1949.

"The night that I won my championship, this weight was lifted off me and I thought, 'This is the greatest feeling ever,'" Lesnar told the *Minneapolis Star Tribune.* "But the next day when I woke up, I never felt so empty inside, because I didn't know what I was going to do now."

One possibility was the upcoming Olympic trials. Lesnar had said during the season that the Olympics were a goal. Another possibility was football. The *Minneapolis Star Tribune* reported that Gophers football coach Glen Mason had talked to Lesnar about playing football for the Gophers in the fall of 2000.

Lesnar soon made a choice. On April 11, the *Minneapolis Star Tribune* reported that Lesnar was near a contract with the World Wrestling Federation. On June 9, the contract was finalized. Lesnar joined a group of former Gophers athletes who went on to professional wrestling— Bronko Nagurski, Gagne, Leo Nomellini, and Shelton Benjamin.

"He's perfectly suited for pro wrestling," Morgan told the newspaper. "He's a farm kid. He has all those skills that come from hard work. He listens well. But he's also a bit of a showman. He loves being a big draw."

On the *Here Comes the Pain* DVD, Lesnar said, "I love to be center-stage, I love to be physical...you know I get that high being out there and being in front of the people and just doing my thing."

The *Figure Four Weekly* newsletter, reported Lesnar had been the focus of a "heated bidding war between New Japan [because he was legit and a monster], WWF [both because of his look and because Kurt Angle had become such a phenom], and WCW [because everyone else wanted him]."

Lesnar told the *Bismarck Tribune* in a 2005 interview that his decision to sign with the WWF was influenced heavily by one factor, "Eighteen years of starving."

Lesnar went on to tell the newspaper that, "It was [a difficult decision]. It really was. Do I stay in school and finish up and play football, since I had another year of eligibility for the Gophers in another sport? Do I go on and follow my dreams as an Olympic wrestler? I locked myself in the basement of the house we were living at for a whole month, because I knew the WWE wanted me. I didn't know what to do. I just made that decision. When I was digging in my pockets to chase my buddies out to grab a beer and a steak or something, and I was digging deep and there was nothing in [them], I said, 'It's time to open a new chapter and see what happens.'"

On August 1, Lesnar began his professional wrestling career when he reported to Louisville, Kentucky, to begin training with Ohio Valley Wrestling—the World Wrestling Federation's development program.

Figure Four Weekly wrote that Lesnar had been given a deal worth several hundred thousand dollars per year when others in the development program were making $500 to $700 per week.

"Even the year before, he [WWF employee Gerald Briscoe] contacted me and talked to me about Brock. I basically said, 'You guys leave him alone. Lay off of him. He's got to wrestle.' They did," said Robinson, who had known Briscoe since college. "They didn't contact him. They didn't do anything to him. You know, I just said, I don't want guys screwing around with him; I don't want guys dealing with him. And after it's over, we'll talk. And after it was over, I kind of helped him put together a deal."

After Lesnar signed with the WWF, Robinson and Briscoe had another conversation.

"I basically told Gerald Briscoe that you guys better take care of him. You better do things right. And they did," Robinson said.

Lesnar's two-year Gophers career left an impression on Robinson and the Gophers' program.

"He worked very hard to get where he was and get the tools that he had. And then when he wrestled in college, he used them to the best of his ability," Robinson said. "And, by that, what I mean is, when he first came here, I tested him right away. You know, because everybody, when you see somebody like that, everybody immediately says steroids. So I tested him. I talked to Brock and we talked about it. And I said, 'Look, I want to test you.' Took him down and tested him. He didn't know it was coming and nothing. I just wanted to be able to say, 'He didn't. Okay?'

"And, so, the beauty of that is one of the things Brock had said stuck with me, and I say it to a lot of people. He said, 'You know everybody had the same opportunity to go in the weight room as I did. They just chose not to do it.' You know, so what he did he chose to go in and do something himself, you know, he obviously had a base to build it, but he went in and put in the time and effort and he was reaping awards. People just want to [think]...have a tendency to [think]...he took a shortcut. He didn't take a shortcut. I think that's the thing that stands out."

DENNIS KOSLOWSKI

Former Olympic wrestler Dennis Koslowski marvels at the number of talented wrestlers that have come out of South Dakota.

"It's amazing," Koslowski said. "There must be something in the [state's] water."

According to 2009 population figures, South Dakota ranked 46th out of the 50 states with a population of just more than 800,000 residents. But during the last 30 years, the state has produced many prominent wrestlers at the national level.

Of the 20 members of the 1988 U.S. Olympic wrestling team, four were from South Dakota—Dennis and Duane Koslowski and Jim and Bill Scherr.

Dennis Koslowski said another South Dakota native played a part in making wrestling popular in the state.

"Randy Lewis [a three-time South Dakota state champion,

two-time NCAA champion, and four-time NCAA All-American at the University of Iowa] graduated [from high school] in 1976," Koslowski said. "He went on to be an Olympic champion [he won a gold medal at the 1984 Olympics]. That was a big step for the whole state. At that time, any guy who wrestled in college was impressive. With four of us on the 1988 team, it had an influence, too. It was important. People could see it was something we could be good at."

Jim Scherr went on to become the CEO of the United States Olympic Committee—the first former Olympic athlete to head the organization.

After high school, Koslowski put together a career that eventually earned him a spot in the National Wrestling Hall of Fame. Koslowski's interest in wrestling started while he was in junior high in Brock Lesnar's hometown of Webster, South Dakota.

"I lived with my grandparents for two years on a farm near Webster," Koslowski said. "The coach [at Webster High School] at the time was a guy named Chuck Scheppy. I learned about wrestling in P.E. class. After he retired, he was replaced by [Gary] Smokey Wallman. He had three sons who were state champions."

After living in Webster, Koslowski went to high school in Doland, South Dakota, (about 60 miles southwest of Webster) where he twice finished in third place at the state meet.

"When I was in high school, I had to wrestle those Webster kids," Koslowski said. "That's the thing, you can't have [an] aversion to hard work. Out in rural areas [like Webster], wrestling is such a tradition. You know in wrestling it's kind of expected that you get thumped the first few years before you make the progression. It's expected you work hard as you gain confidence."

Koslowski, who along with Smokey Wallman was inducted into the South Dakota Athletic Hall of Fame in April 2010, said he saw similarities between himself and Lesnar.

"I think in some ways Brock is like me," Koslowski said. "I never won a state title, either. I went from 105 pounds to 167 pounds in high school, moving up two or three weights a year. In college I went from 177 pounds to heavyweight. In international competition, I wrestled at 220 pounds. That was the best weight for me."

After high school, Koslowski and his twin brother, Duane, attended the University of Minnesota–Morris. While in college, Koslowski was introduced to Greco-Roman wrestling.

"A big reason I got into it was because of Brad Rheingans," Koslowski said. "He was from [nearby] Appleton [Minnesota], and he came up to Morris over Christmas break to work out with us. He was on the 1976 and 1980 Olympic teams. He was third at the World Championships in 1979. We became good friends. He didn't get to compete at the 1980 Olympics because of the [U.S.] boycott, so he went into pro wrestling."

Rheingans tried to convince Koslowski to go into pro wrestling.

"He always felt that if I knew and met the guys [in pro wrestling] that I would want to be a part of it," Koslowski said. "But it actually had an opposite effect on me. I didn't like the entertainer lifestyle. And I had other options."

After being named all-conference in football three times (as an offensive lineman) and earning two NCAA Division III wrestling titles, Koslowski graduated from Minnesota–Morris in 1982. Koslowski passed up pro wrestling to attend chiropractor school. While attending school, Koslowski began training in Greco-Roman (a style of wrestling that forbids holds below the waist).

"He [Rheingans] came down to the Twin Cities for training, and we were roommates for awhile," Koslowski said.

In 1983, Koslowski won his first national title and went on to win seven national titles in Greco-Roman and compete in the World Championships five times. He was an alternate to the 1984 U.S. Olympic team before winning a bronze medal at the 1988 Olympics in Seoul and a silver medal at the 1992 Olympics in Barcelona.

In 1990 he started his own chiropractic practice in Minneapolis, and he retired from wrestling after the 1992 Olympic Games. But he still followed wrestling. In the fall of 1997, he heard about a junior college wrestler in North Dakota.

"The first I knew of Brock, he was at Bismarck," Koslowski said. "The Gophers start their year every year at the Bison Open [in Fargo, North Dakota]. That year they won 9-of-10 [individual] titles at the Open, and the only one they didn't win, Brock won.

"The Gophers had Brock come down to Minneapolis on a recruiting trip. The first time I met him, I was working out in the Gophers wrestling room with [former Gophers heavyweight] Billy Pierce, who was an assistant coach at the time and was trying to make the Olympics. Brock came down into the room, and I shook hands with him."

Koslowski followed Lesnar's career at the University of Minnesota and followed his career after Lesnar joined the WWE (WWF at the time) in 2000.

"I think Rheingans helped Brock when he was in pro wrestling," Koslowski said. "I'm sure they still talk. I think because of their amateur backgrounds they developed a friendship. Brad was the most mild-mannered guy [outside of the ring]."

Koslowski wasn't surprised when Lesnar chose to leave the WWE in 2004. "I remember driving in to work a few months before he left the WWE," Koslowski said. "I heard him do an interview on [Minnesota radio station] KFAN. He sounded depressed and sounded like he hated the lifestyle. I think he had come to the realization it was time to leave."

After Koslowski had competed in the 1992 Olympics, he briefly fought professionally in Japan.

"I did a year of shoot fighting [combat sport] in Japan in 1992 and 1993 after the 1992 Olympics," Koslowski said. "I got a call from the UFC to see if I was interested, but I said no."

Koslowski pointed out that several former Greco-Roman wrestlers went on to fight in MMA and UFC. "Randy Couture, he was always a weight below me," Koslowski said. "He was a good Greco-Roman wrestler. His timing was perfect. He wrestled through 1996, before he joined UFC. Also, [light heavyweight] Dan Henderson, who was on the 1992 and 1996 Olympic teams."

Since 2007, Koslowski has been the team chiropractor for the Minnesota Vikings. Vikings linebacker Chad Greenway has provided Koslowski a reminder of his wrestling background.

"Chad grew up in [Mount Vernon] South Dakota and attended Iowa," Koslowski said. "He's a big wrestling guy. I met has did last fall [2009]. His dad said he wrestled in high school, and I kind of did the math. And, I think we wrestled when he was in high school."

WES HAND

One of the highlights of the NCAA Division I wrestling regular season is the annual National Duals.

In 1999, perennial powerhouse Iowa played host to the two-day event. The host Hawkeyes, who won eight NCAA wrestling championships in the 1990s, faced the University of Minnesota, a program on the rise, in the semifinals.

Wrestling for Minnesota at heavyweight was a relatively unknown junior named Brock Lesnar, who was in his first month of eligibility for the Gophers. Iowa heavyweight Wes Hand, who was an All-America selection the previous season as a sophomore, didn't know much about his opponent. But during the next 15 months, Hand would get to know Lesnar pretty well.

"I knew pretty much nothing about him," Hand said. "I heard a name. I heard some rumors that Minnesota had a big, huge guy at heavyweight. But other than that, I hardly knew anything at all about him."

Going into his first match against Lesnar, Hand was having a good junior season.

"I was doing well," Hand said. "I think I had lost only once at that point. I was doing pretty good. A lot of teams have good heavyweights. I knew what I was up against."

Lesnar, who had won his first two matches at the meet by pin, pinned the 6'1", 240-pound Hand in 2:36 to help the Gophers defeat the Hawkeyes 21–14.

"You really don't know what you're up against until you actually feel it," Hand said. "The first time he hit me with a double-leg, I was thinking, 'Holy cow, I'm in a battle. This isn't normal.'

"I'm not a weak guy. I consider myself a pretty strong, powerful guy. He planted me on my back, and I knew then what I was up against. I was kind of shell-shocked. Not to the point that I couldn't wrestle, but at that point, I hadn't been blasted like that before."

The two met again two weeks later in a dual meet in Iowa City.

"That match was a lot different," Hand said. "I knew what to expect. I really felt prepared."

Lesnar, who had jumped to No. 2 in the national heavyweight rankings after his undefeated performance at the National Duals, defeated Hand 6–0 to help the Gophers pull out a 19–17 victory over the Hawkeyes.

"The match was close until late in the match," Hand said. "He shot and rolled me back on my ankle. I couldn't do much on my ankle after that, and I never really recovered that season.

"But coming out of that match, even though I had lost, I thought I had made significant gains. I thought there were some positions that gave me some chances for the next time."

The two did not wrestle again that season.

The next meeting between Hand and Lesnar, who had gone on to win the Big Ten title and finish as the runner-up at the NCAA meet, occurred in the next season.

On February 20, 2000, the Gophers, ranked No. 2 in the nation, and the Hawkeyes, ranked No. 1, closed out the regular season with a dual meet in Minneapolis.

Going into the heavyweight match between Hand and Lesnar, the Hawkeyes trailed the Gophers 13–10. Hand silenced the crowd of 13,128 by handing Lesnar a 5–3 defeat—Lesnar's first and only loss of the season. Iowa went on to win the dual 20–13.

"To be honest, I was pretty jacked up," Hand said. "I think I had won 20 in a row. I'd only had one bad match all year. I'd had a year to sit on [our] matches from the previous year. I was embarrassed and knew I hadn't wrestled well. And it was the final dual meet of our careers. So my mentality was, I was really fired up. I went into the match confident that I could beat him."

Hand surprised Lesnar with a takedown and near-fall in the first period to take a 4–0 lead.

"The move that I hit on him to get ahead," Hand said, "was one I practiced all the time. Whip-over, pancake, whatever you want to call it. It maybe took him by surprise."

After taking the early 4–0 lead, Hand had to avoid mistakes and hang on.

"The rest of the match, neither one of us had a takedown," Hand said. "I was a little bigger and stronger than the previous year. I was probably, 248-250 pounds.

"What I remember most about that night and will remember for the rest of my life was there was a guy in the stands, right next to where I was warming up before my match. He was yelling at me, 'Don't show up Hand. You're going to get your *blank* kicked.' I pretty much ignored him. After I won the match, I was about 5 feet from him, and all I said to him was, 'Really?'"

Hand said the atmosphere in the University of Minnesota's Williams Arena that night "was the best I wrestled in. Minnesota did a good job of ramping up the crowd and getting them into the match. When we trained at Iowa, our attitude was, 'It's us against the world.' And it was that night. There was a little corner of the arena with Iowa fans; the rest were for Minnesota. It was really awesome. It was the best athletic atmosphere I've ever been in."

Two weeks later, Hand and Lesnar renewed their rivalry at the Big Ten Tournament. In the heavyweight championship, Lesnar outlasted Hand 2–1 to win his second conference title.

"I think Brock had a little advantage over me in the top position because he's a big, strong guy," Hand said. "I was really cautious about getting underneath him. The difference in our match at the Big Ten was I was still cautious and he was really cautious, too. That match was probably boring for the fans. There was not a lot going on. He didn't do much, and neither did I until the end of the match when I was behind."

They met in St. Louis—at the NCAA championship two weeks later—for their final match.

"Going into the match at nationals, I felt confident," Hand said. "I had beat him once and lost a close one. I felt he had some small weaknesses. At the end of the match at Big Tens, I took a shot at his legs. I kind of felt he headed to the edge of the mat. That he didn't want a part of it. I felt something mentally."

Their NCAA championship match was a mirror of their Big Ten championship match, as Lesnar pulled out a 3–2 victory in a tiebreaker.

"I've told this story 200 times," Hand said. "I wrestled way better against him at Nationals than I did in the match when I beat him. I felt I was the aggressor. It came down to a coin flip [in the tiebreaker]. I had some positions I didn't take advantage of. It came down to 30 seconds. I had to ride him out. He escaped with about 10 seconds to go."

Ten years later, Hand's matches against Lesnar are still being brought up.

"I [still] get asked about our matches a lot," Hand said. "What I say is the first time we wrestled, he overwhelmed me. Truthfully, as a junior he was better than me. As a senior, not so much. We had some tight matches. He is so strong, so athletic. It takes so much strategy [just] to stay in the match against him. You have to. He's got so much strength, speed, and athletic ability."

After graduating from Iowa, Hand spent four seasons as an assistant wrestling coach at Virginia Tech before returning to Iowa as an assistant. After two seasons, Hand left to become a sales representative in Eastern Iowa for a medical supply company.

"It wasn't a hard decision," said the Tama, Iowa, native. "It was the right time to exit the program and the sport. I'm ambitious and wanted to try other things."

Living in Davenport, Iowa, Hand is a UFC fan. "I am absolutely," Hand said. "I'm a fan of the UFC and of Brock. I text him occasionally, and we communicate from time to time. I'm a supporter of Brock.

"We talked briefly about me coming up to help him train for a fight, but it didn't work out mainly because of my schedule. He and I are on good terms. I wish him the best and hope he keeps on winning."

CHAPTER 5

THE NEXT BIG THING

The World Wrestling Federation (WWF) hadn't been Lesnar's goal, but it made him an offer he couldn't refuse. Lesnar, who passed up an opportunity to train for the U.S. Olympic team, told the Associated Press, "Joining the WWF was not [my] dream, but the decision would benefit [my] family."

After signing with the WWF, Lesnar lamented the lack of opportunities for wrestlers after college.

"Oh yes, that definitely bothers me," Lesnar told the Associated Press, "but what can you do? You know that when you start wrestling that there isn't anything besides the Olympics after college where you can go out and excel."

On August 1, 2000, Lesnar reported to Louisville, Kentucky, to join Ohio Valley Wrestling (OVW)—the WWF's talent development program. When Lesnar joined OVW, it was known as "Off Broadway" on the professional wrestling circuit. OVW, which was founded by Danny Davis in 1998, had become part of WWF's development program earlier in the year.

"It's just what I'm looking for," Lesnar told the Associated Press. "I like the business. I like the people, and I want to be a wrestler."

Gerald Briscoe told the WWF's website that Lesnar "will easily find success in professional wrestling. I think he'll be one of those guys that comes in and is a natural. I think the world of the guy. He can be compared to Kurt Angle. I think he'll be as good [as] or better than Kurt. He's only 22, so he's got a lot of time to grow."

On the *Here Comes the Pain* DVD, Briscoe recalled, "The minute Brock Lesnar walked off the mat in St. Louis, Missouri, where he won his national championship, I knew this guy would be a long-term guy. Anybody that he steps in the ring with, he can elevate just by his intensity. When I recruited Brock, we had an event in Minneapolis and Brock came down to the event. Vince McMahon walked by, and Vince asked Brock, 'Are you ready to be in the WWE?' And Brock says, 'I've always wanted to entertain people.' And I knew that was the right answer."

In a December 2000 article, the *Louisville Courier-Journal* described Ohio Valley Wrestling, "Located in a scruffy, Civil War–era warehouse in Jefferson, Indiana (on the other side of the Ohio River from Louisville), Ohio Valley Wrestling is a learning laboratory, a bona fide educational institution where raw recruits come to learn the business of drop kicks and power slams. From this, the Harvard of the Headlock, could one day come the next 'Stone Cold' Steve Austin or Jerry 'The King' Lawler."

The article went on to describe the school as "a tag-team operation, with [Jim] Cornette handling the show biz side, and his longtime friend—and OVW founder—Danny Davis teaching the wrestling moves and tricks picked up during two decades in the ring."

Davis started his career in professional wrestling in the early 1980s as a referee. In 1987, he became a wrestler. Using the name "Dangerous" Danny Davis, the 6', 180-pounder took part in Wrestlemania III and IV and the first two events in the Survivor Series as a member of the Hart Foundation. He returned to refereeing in 1989, which he continued until the mid-1990s.

According to the newspaper, Davis "opened the school seven years ago, after his body told him to retire and his now ex-wife suggested they settle in Louisville, her hometown [Davis is a Delaware native]. It took off from there, morphing into a full-blown wrestling operation with a weekly TV show and a crew of wrestlers barnstorming all over [Kentucky]."

Cornette was described in the article as understanding the pro wrestling business "as well as anyone, maybe even as well as WWF head Vince McMahon. He knows what works, and he knows what to discard. He knows the audience, and he knows exactly what to give them night after night."

Cornette described himself to the newspaper as "the classic hanger-on."

As a young boy, Cornette had watched wrestling at the Louisville Gardens. He got his first job in pro wrestling at 15. He had jobs as a manager, promoter, and announcer before getting hired as a talent scout for the WWE.

Cornette told the newspaper, "The perfect wrestler is someone who is equal parts athlete, actor, acrobat, and comedian. The thing is, wrestling is the oldest form of combat known. The caveman wrestled. And everyone in the American public can understand that. Two guys are going to get into the ring and wrestle. Who's gonna win?"

Figure Four Weekly, an online newsletter, wrote, "Jim Cornette ordered fifteen copies of Lou Thesz's book *Hooker* to hand out to the guys in Ohio Valley as a textbook of sorts. Just listening to various stories, Ohio Valley sounds like the place to be for a young wrestler who really wants to learn the business. They work four to six days a week. Cornette is a total stickler for kayfabe [the portrayal of pro wrestling as real] and has an old-school mentality that really teaches a respect for the business that a lot of older wrestlers feel the guys coming up today don't have. He also reportedly hands out a four-tape study set of classic wrestling matches, which comes complete with a stack of notes pointing out what the student should look for and be aware of in each of the matches. He's also got trainers there like Danny Davis, Rip Rogers, and Bobby Eaton to help teach a guy anything in the world there is to learn about wrestling. It's a success, too, because you can actually see the guys improving week by week on the TV."

Davis told the *Louisville Courier-Journal*, "Years ago, I realized that Jimmy was a genius. I knew that he was gonna get tired of traveling the world and would one day want to come home. I knew that if I had something to offer him, we could pair up."

At the time Cornette was looking to return to Louisville, Davis was looking to expand OVW.

According to the newspaper, "Impressed with Davis' no-frills operation, Cornette approached his bosses with a proposal to turn Ohio Valley Wrestling into, for a lack of a better term, a minor-league affiliate of the WWF. It would be a full-service shop where young wrestlers could learn the ropes and veteran stars could come to recover from injuries. The bosses liked the idea, and in July 1999, the OVW became an official affiliate of the World Wrestling Federation. Training sessions are loose and spirited with Davis jumping in and out of the ring to show, rather than just tell, how things are done. This has earned him a measure of respect from his pupils."

Not long after he joined Ohio Valley Wrestling, Lesnar suffered a temporary setback when a knee injury sidelined him. But after returning to the mat, Lesnar was re-united with a familiar face—Shelton Benjamin—to form a tag team called the Minnesota Stretching Crew.

"I've known him [Benjamin] for years," Lesnar told the *Minnesota Daily*. "I've worked out with him a number of times. He and I pretty much have the same mentality. I've asked him a lot of questions. He loves it. So I'm assuming I will, too. I know I will."

Benjamin had been with Ohio Valley Wrestling for sixth months.

The *Louisville Courier-Journal* described Benjamin as "an amazing physical specimen—tall, strong, cut from granite—but blessed with amazing agility. One moment, he may be diving onto an opponent from the top rope of the ring; the next he will be using that same rope to perform an impromptu high-wire act, oblivious to the concrete floor 10 feet below."

Benjamin told the newspaper that the transition from college to pro wrestling was difficult. "For me, getting into the ring and learning the moves wasn't hard. The hardest part was learning to get beat. I don't think I'll ever get used to that. But I'm not here to win or lose, I'm here to entertain."

Like Lesnar, Benjamin was a former junior college and University of Minnesota heavyweight and a newcomer to OVW. Benjamin, 25, spent the previous year as an assistant coach at the University of Minnesota where he worked out with Lesnar.

The 6'2", 250-pound Benjamin was a two-time All-America selection for the Gophers. Benjamin, a native of Orangeburg, South Carolina, joined the Gophers in 1996 after two seasons at Lassen Junior College in Susanville, California. Benjamin, who had won two South Carolina heavyweight state championships in high school, won the NJCAA heavyweight championship in 1996. Later that year, Benjamin won the NJCAA 100-meter championship.

In his first season with the Gophers, Benjamin compiled a 25–16 record and finished fifth at the NCAA meet. In his senior season, he went 36–6 with 12 pins. He was the runner-up at the Big Ten meet before going 6–1 and finishing third at the NCAA meet in Cleveland. Like Lesnar, Benjamin bypassed a chance to try out for the 2000 Olympics by turning professional.

As a tag team, Benjamin and Lesnar were an immediate success. *Figure Four Weekly*, an online newsletter devoted to wrestling, predicted that Benjamin and Lesnar would eventually be big stars.

On February 13, 2001, about 6-1/2 months after joining OVW, Lesnar teamed with Benjamin to defeat the Disciples of Synn (B.J. Payne and Damien) to claim the OVW Southern Tag Team title for the first time. Two months later, Payne and Damien reclaimed the title from Lesnar and Benjamin. On May 15, the Minnesota Stretching Crew reclaimed the title from Payne and Damien.

On June 27, in front of about 3,000 fans at the Louisville Gardens, Lesnar and Brian Keck, who was filling in for the injured Benjamin, defeated Perry Saturn and Dean Malenko to retain the tag team title. But in July, because of Benjamin's injury (which would sideline him for five months), the Minnesota Stretching Crew was stripped of the title.

On September 26, Lesnar sat ringside during the taping of OVW's weekly television show and watched Rico Constantino and The Prototype John Cena defeat Payne and Damien for the tag team title. Lesnar got involved in the match and displayed his strength by carrying Kenny Bolin to the back after Bolin tried to interfere with the match.

A week later, during the October 3 taping, it was announced that Payne and Damien would wrestle Lesnar and Benjamin, with the winner of that match to face Constantino and The Prototype for the tag team title. On the same show, Constantino defeated Lesnar. The taping marked the return of Benjamin to action as he showed up when Bolin tried to interfere with the Constantino/Lesnar match.

In early October, the WWF began split-crew tours and occasionally called up OVW wrestlers for the events. Lesnar was called up to be part of a crew in Winnipeg, Manitoba, on October 5 and in St. Paul, Minnesota, on October 6. Among those featured on the October 6 card in St. Paul were Kurt Angle, Chris Jericho, and Stone Cold Steve Austin.

Lesnar told the *Minneapolis Star Tribune* he was still learning.

"It was strange at first," Lesnar said. "I don't know really how to explain it. It's kind of night and day. The competitiveness is there. The whole performing thing has been fun."

Lesnar added that he did not regret bypassing a chance at the Olympics at join the WWF.

"I'm fortunate. Wrestling heavyweight and looking the way I do, I'm grateful," Lesnar said. "A lot of smaller guys don't have the opportunity. A lot of people don't like their jobs. I do."

In an interview with the *Bismarck Tribune* in June 2005, Lesnar recalled his professional wrestling beginnings, "I had to go in with an open mind, keep [my mouth] shut and my ears open. They didn't stick me out in the ring. I trained for a year and a half, every single day. I committed to myself. I committed to Vince McMahon, and I wanted to be a pro wrestler. From the day I signed on the dotted line, I turned that switch, and I just wanted to become an entertainer. I go the same feeling out of it as I did as an amateur wrestling."

WWF senior vice president for talent relations Jim Ross, the primary announcer on WWF broadcasts, told the *Minneapolis Star Tribune* that Lesnar, "is one of the top physical specimens [I] have ever seen."

To become a star in the WWF, Ross said Lesnar would have to work on his showmanship. "We know he can deliver the steak. We have to work on his sizzle. Your governor [Jesse Ventura] was long on sizzle. He needs to take a page from your governor's book and enhance his charisma. But it's not uncommon at all. And it's not a big concern."

During the October 17 OVW taping, Lesnar, Benjamin, and Val Venis defeated Payne, Damien, and Leviathan when Venis pinned the 6'5", 317-pound Leviathan.

On October 30, during a WWF RAW taping in Louisville, Lesnar and Benjamin reclaimed the tag-team title by defeating Constantino and Prototype. The match was the first "dark match" for Lesnar and Benjamin. The next night, during the OVW taping, Lesnar and Benjamin defeated Jason Lee and Derrick King to retain the title. During the November 14 OVW taping, Lesnar and Benjamin again defeated Payne and Damien.

In late December, Ross mentioned Lesnar and Benjamin in his weekly report on the WWF website. Ross wrote that among the OVW wrestlers the WWF continued to look at for a "call-up" were Lesnar, Benjamin, and The Prototype John Cena. Ross wrote, "It seems as if Prototype and Benjamin are at the top of the list" of those potentially being brought up in 2002.

Throughout late 2001 and early 2002, Lesnar continued to split his time between OVW shows and WWF split-tour "house shows" and "dark matches."

In mid-February, Ross wrote in his weekly report that Lesnar "had a concussion." A couple of weeks later, Ross wrote that Lesnar was "looking good."

In mid-March on an episode of RAW, Lesnar finally made his WWF television debut. Lesnar was accompanied by Paul Heyman, who was brought back as an "old-style" manager to speak for Lesnar. On the episode, Lesnar and Heyman, who had previously been a manager for Steve Austin and several other high-profile wrestlers, got involved in a Hardcore match, attacking Spike Dudley, Maven, and Al Snow. Three days later, Lesnar interrupted a match between Hurricane and Molly—beating them both.

One week after his television debut, Lesnar—and Heyman, who was the first to label Lesnar as "The Next Big Thing"—defeated Rikishi, a 6'1", 420-pound Samoan. Following that match, Lesnar was "drafted" by Ric Flair for the WWF RAW brand.

The WWF had been considering a draft for nearly a year, almost immediately after the WWF purchased World Championship Wrestling (WCW) from Time Warner/AOL in early 2001. The WWF didn't think that the WCW would be able to stand on its own, so it decided to combine the rosters of the two organizations and split the company (via draft) into two brands. WWF thought this would lead to an entertaining feud between the two brands. A draft was originally scheduled for July 2001, but it was repeatedly rescheduled.

The draft was finally held on March 25, when Flair's RAW and Vince McMahon's Smackdown franchises each drafted 20 wrestlers. The rest of the performers were assigned to one of the franchises by a lottery.

Lesnar quickly became a standout for the RAW brand. On March 27 in Wilkes-Barre, Pennsylvania, Lesnar defeated Spike. The next night in East Rutherford, New Jersey, Lesnar defeated Spike and Hurricane in a handicap match.

April was a hectic month for Lesnar. It included his first "feud" and the birth of his first child.

On the April 1 RAW, the Hardy Boyz defeated Mr. Perfect and Bossman when Lesnar entered the ring and beat up the Hardy Boyz. At a house show in Reading, Pennsylvania, the next night, Lesnar defeated Spike with an airplane spin finish. Later in the show, Lesnar ran out to attack Justin "Hawk" Bradshaw, who had just defeated Credible, but Bradshaw, a 6'6" 300-pound Texan, was able to fight off Lesnar.

On the April 8 episode of RAW, Lesnar was attacked by the Hardy Boyz and withstood two chair shots without leaving his feet.

On April 13, WWF made a stop in Odessa, Texas, for the first time in 11 years. The crowd saw Lesnar defeat Bradshaw. A week later, in Des Moines, Iowa, Lesnar defeated Jeff Hardy when the referee stopped the match.

On April 21, 2002, four days after the birth of his daughter, Lesnar squared off against Jeff Hardy in a Backlash pay-per-view event from Kemper Arena in Kansas City, Missouri. The match was stopped by the referee and credited as a knockout victory for Lesnar. The next night on RAW, it was the same result for Lesnar against Matt Hardy, the other half of the Hardy Boyz.

In early May, the WWF sent a crew to England and Scotland. On May 2, in Glasgow, Scotland, Lesnar pinned Matt Hardy. Two days later, at London's Wembley Stadium, Lesnar and Shawn Stasiak were defeated by the Hardy Boyz. The London event, billed as the Insurrextion pay-per-view, was the last television show to be aired under the WWF name. On the May 6 episode of RAW, the organization started using the World Wrestling Entertainment (WWE) name.

But the most talked about portion of the excursion to England was the group's return trip to the United States. According to the *Figure Four Weekly* online newsletter, the charter flight home was marred by several altercations, one which reportedly included Lesnar and Curt Hennig. Hennig, a Minnesota native who had been trained by Minnesota professional wrestling legend Verne Gagne, reportedly challenged Lesnar to a wrestling match in the aisle and kept goading Lesnar over who had the best amateur wrestling skills. Eventually the two had to be separated. Hennig, who was also known as "Mr. Perfect," was fired by the company the next day (May 5). Hennig went to work for Total Nonstop Action Wrestling (TNA), but less than a year later, he died at the age of 44. Hennig, described by the WWE as "one of the best in-ring technicians of his generation," was inducted into the WWE Hall of Fame in 2007.

On the May 13 episode of RAW, Lesnar lost to the Hardy Boyz by disqualification. Less than a week later—on the Judgment Day pay-per-view event—Lesnar and Heyman defeated the Hardy Boyz, when Lesnar tagged off and Heyman pinned Jeff Hardy. That same week, in Louisville, Lesnar defeated D-Lo.

In early June, Lesnar defeated Bubba Dudley in a King of the Ring qualifying match. A week later, Lesnar won his King of the Ring quarterfinal match over Booker T, who had been a 10-time WCW World Tag Team champion with his brother Stevie Ray. On June 23, Lesnar defeated Test in the semifinals and Rob Van Dam, a former ECW champion who was in his first year in the WWE, in the finals to win the King of the Ring championship. That gave him a berth in the WWE Undisputed Championship match at the upcoming SummerSlam.

In late July, Van Dam defeated Lesnar by disqualification to win the WWE Intercontinental title. The next night on RAW, Lesnar defeated Tommy Dreamer in a Singapore Cane match. After the match, Lesnar surprised RAW General Manager Eric Bischoff by saying he was joining Stephanie McMahon's Smackdown brand. Three days later, the Smackdown episode included a segment with Lesnar telling Kurt Angle that his days as the top wrestler on Smackdown were over. On the August 8 Smackdown, Lesnar defeated legend Hulk Hogan.

On August 25 on the SummerSlam pay-per-view event, with his parents in attendance, Lesnar defeated The Rock to become, at age 25, the youngest WWE Undisputed Champion. It had taken Lesnar less than a year to reach the pinnacle of professional wrestling. Vince McMahon liked to say that it took 18 months to create a star. According to *Figure Four Weekly*, "It didn't take 18 months to create Brock Lesnar; it took one summer of great booking."

Lesnar recalled the memorable day for the *Here Comes the Pain* DVD. "My emotions going into that day and that night and that match was I knew that this was going to be a big career change for me and a big step in my career. How it came to be for my parents to be at SummerSlam, my parents are my number one fans, they always travel with me, they used to take me to little kids wrestling tournaments every Saturday, they followed me throughout my whole career. I wanted them to be a part of this also and instead of watching me on television to be at the actual live event."

Stephanie Lesnar recalled for the DVD, "I was right in the match, well every time he did something great I was right there with him. I think we connected eyes; our eyes connected a couple of times."

Richard Lesnar said, "Well, the crowd was into it, my stomach just got, it just kind of got nervous and tight and my mouth got dry. It was exciting, and they went right at it."

Stephanie Lesnar said she thought the crowd got behind her son. "It seemed like they kind of switched over to Brock instead of The Rock."

Brock said, "I first noticed when the crowd got behind me was when I got Rock in the bearhug, the Brock Lock. I felt the fans really anticipated that Brock Lesnar is going to win this match. When I won, the first thing that went through my mind was that I had to take it all in. This was the number one goal for every professional wrestler is to have the WWE Championship, and I have it and I've achieved it in a short amount of time. It really hasn't even sunk in yet. When I saw my parents backstage, for them to come up and congratulate me, and my mom was shaking and smiling, it brought back memories from when I won my NCAA title and my junior college title. I wanted them to be a part of it, and that's why I brought them to SummerSlam. That match made Brock Lesnar."

Bischoff expected Lesnar to return to RAW the night after SummerSlam, but Stephanie McMahon announced that Lesnar's contract only required him to defend the title on Smackdown. Bischoff created the World Heavyweight Championship for the RAW brand and awarded it to Triple H, meaning there was no longer an undisputed WWE world champion.

On September 4, OVW did its first taping from its new facility in Louisville, and the show included many WWE wrestlers. The main event was scheduled to be Lesnar against Doug Basham for the WWE title. As the taping opened, Jim Ross announced that the scheduled main event between Lesnar and Basham would not take place because Lesnar had suffered an elbow injury against the Undertaker. Lesnar was replaced by Chris Benoit.

Two days later, the RAW crew was in Sioux Falls, South Dakota—150 miles from Lesnar's hometown of Webster. Lesnar was brought in for the event and faced Hunter in a RAW-Smackdown title match. A crowd of more than 6,000 cheered Lesnar as he beat Hunter with an F–5.

The Sioux Falls event began a busy stretch for Lesnar. The next night the Smackdown crew was in Washington, D.C., as Lesnar defeated the Undertaker. The following night in Cleveland, it was the same result as Lesnar defeated the Undertaker again. On September 9, Smackdown traveled to Mankato, Minnesota, where Lesnar and Kurt Angle had their first WWE match. Lesnar defeated the 1996 Olympic gold medalist (in freestyle wrestling) with the F–5.

On September 15, the crew was in Billings, Montana, where Lesnar defeated the 6'5", 250-pound Edge with the F–5 to keep his WWE title. The match reportedly stopped for five minutes after a fan threw a full beverage cup at Lesnar.

On the September 19 Smackdown, after Lesnar had defeated John Cena, who had been an NCAA Division III football All-American for Springfield (Massachusetts) College, in a non-title match, the feud between Lesnar and the Undertaker continued as the two brawled at the end of the show.

Four nights later, on the Unforgiven pay-per-view, the Lesnar-Undertaker match ended in disqualification, a result which disappointed many of the pay-per-view customers. *Figure Four Weekly* reported that Lesnar was disappointed in the finish because "he was brought up under the Jim Cornette/OVW training system where matches of this magnitude didn't have such horrendous finishes."

One night after Unforgiven, Lesnar pinned Edge in Santa Barbara, California, to retain his title.

On October 3 the Smackdown crew was in Lafayette, Louisiana, and Lesnar attacked the Undertaker after his match by hitting him with a propane tank. The Undertaker reportedly suffered a broken hand.

The feud with the Undertaker culminated with Lesnar beating the 6'10", 295-pound Undertaker in a Hell in the Cell match on the No Mercy event on October 20. On October 26 on the Rebellion pay-per-view event, Lesnar retained the undisputed title when he (along with Heyman) beat Edge in a handicap match.

Storylines for the rest of 2002 had Lesnar feuding with The Big Show and Kurt Angle and a "suspension." On the November 17 Survivor series, the Big Show, with help from Heyman, defeated Lesnar to claim the Undisputed Title.

On Smackdown four days after that loss, Lesnar went against Stephanie McMahon's wishes and attacked the Undertaker. Lesnar was "suspended" for his actions. The suspension was lifted about a month later, when Lesnar defeated Shannon Moore on the December 19 Smackdown.

It had been an eventful year for Lesnar. *Pro Wrestling Illustrated*, in its "Year in Review" for 2002 (which was published in April 2003), named Lesnar its Wrestler of the Year and Most Improved Wrestler of the Year.

The recognition from *Pro Wrestling Illustrated* came despite that the magazine, according to its publisher Stu Saks, had "screwed up" by not listing Lesnar on the ballot in the December 2002 issue. Saks wrote in the recap issue, "Once the issue was printed, we could only hope that our readers would take it upon themselves to choose Brock as a write-in candidate so the Wrestler of the Year award would go to the man who deserved it most."

In the Wrestler of the Year poll, Lesnar received 48 percent of the votes to finish ahead of Rob Van Dam (18 percent), Triple H (16 percent), and the Undertaker (10 percent).

Pro Wrestling Illustrated pointed out, "Ironically, just two weeks before the deadline for the PWI achievements awards, Lesnar was upset by "Show" at Survivor Series. That loss [Lesnar's only televised single loss of the year] didn't impact voters much as Lesnar cruised to win Wrestler of the Year by the largest margin in any category. Not bad considering Lesnar wasn't even listed as a top candidate on the original ballot.

"The fact that Lesnar was a runaway winner, garnering 48 percent of the vote to runner-up Van Dam's 18 percent, proved what a dominant year Brock [had]. In this year's voting, Lesnar's margin of victory in the Wrestler of the Year category was only eclipsed by his margin of victory in the Most Improved Wrestler, where the second-year superstar scored 61 percent of the votes to Trish Stratus' 14 percent."

Lesnar was the first wrestler in the magazine's history to simultaneously be tabbed the top vote-getter in both categories.

The issue recapped Lesnar's year: "Last year at this time, the relatively few fans who knew who Brock Lesnar was knew him as a tag-team specialist. Lesnar and Shelton Benjamin comprised the Minnesota Stretching Crew, one of the most popular tandems in Ohio

Valley Wrestling. Even then it was apparent Lesnar had a world of potential—and then some. The former NCAA wrestling champion was huge and athletic, and he was just getting into the game. The 295-pounder's 'shooting star press' quickly became *the* 'you've-got-to-see-it-to-believe-it' high spot in the territory.

"Yet despite all that potential, there were chinks in Lesnar's heavy armor. He sometimes seemed overwhelmed by the transition from the amateur mats to the pro ring, occasionally looking lost inside the squared circle. He seemed unsure of how to follow up on successful maneuvers and had difficulty with the likes of Payne and Damien. In fact, many fans perceived Benjamin as the one who carried the Stretching Crew at times. In 2002, the perception changed. Ironically, Lesnar's improvement came as he scaled back on his offensive repertoire.

"Lesnar abandoned his aerial skills almost entirely and cut back on his amateur takedowns and chain wrestling. He developed and perfected the F–5, perhaps the most effective finisher in wrestling today. The amateur standout became a brawling powerhouse and he dominated WWE as few other others have ever done—and he did it through sheer brutality."

The publication concluded by saying Lesnar was good for WWE. "At a time when World Wrestling Entertainment needed a boost, Lesnar strapped on his Minnesota working boots and became the promotion's No. 1 attraction and did so in classic 'stone-cold' fashion. Instead of playing to the crowd, Lesnar did what he's paid to do: kick ass. When fans started cheering, it wasn't because he was shoved down their throats, it was because they wanted to. Big difference.

"In a matter of months, Lesnar went from 'dark matches' against Crash Holly to pay-per-view main events. He toppled The Rock, grounded RVD [Rob Van Dam], humbled The Undertaker in a Hell in a Cell bloodbath, and left Hulk Hogan a broken and bloody mess in the center of the ring. That's an improvement that can't be overlooked. 2002 saw [Lesnar] live up to his 'Next Big Thing' label."

One way Lesnar had become the Next Big Thing was his work ethic. He described his training regime on the *Here Comes the Pain* DVD. "In my mind I'm No. 1, always. I wouldn't be here if I didn't feel like I was No. 1. For me, I've always trained in little hole-in-the-wall gyms, and that's how I liked it. It wasn't easy for me to get to town, so I just had to use my imagination.

"The exercise I do with the sticks is basically just a good warm-up routine, and it works your shoulders, your back, your chest, all kinds of different areas, and it works on your flexibility.

"It's a normal gym routine to do a step-up with weights on your back or dumbbells in your hands, with a log on my back, it's kind of like me throwing another guy around—a 180-pound log, it works the whole body.

"Fighting the handbag, for me, that was just working on my hand-eye coordination and cardio. That's the only thing that's going through my mind right there is just kicking the crap out of my opponent.

"I got tired of doing pushups on the ground, so I brought chairs into it, me being above the ground, I could go a lot deeper and I didn't have the ground stopping me, I'd always finish up my chest workout with push-ups.

"The sit-up drill that I do is basically an amateur drill that I learned at a very young age, it works on mat quickness and speed and agility on the mat. If you've got strong hips and you're quick on the mat, you're lethal.

"You can do a lot of different things with the rubber bands, I did normal hand movements with the rubber bands, and it just puts resistance on it. I would hold the rubber bands in and take my double-leg shot and it puts resistance on me, and hold it close to your hips it works on your hip speed again.

"For me to take ice baths, get me in that ice water, number one: it's a mental thing. The water is 35 degrees; it's no different than putting an ice bag on your elbow. When you jump in the ice bath, it's your whole body. If you can sit in there for 10–12 minutes, you've broken the mental stage of it and now it's a physical thing. I'm recuperating my body, reviving my muscles for the next day of training.

"I've always got the mindset of beating my opponent, every repetition is for my opponent, you know? Get one more for him. I've got to train like a mad man all year long, makes me that much better, outdo my opponent, always."

On January 19, 2003, Lesnar defeated the Big Show to earn a spot in the Royal Rumble. Lesnar entered the Royal Rumble as the No. 29 entrant and eventually defeated the Undertaker to win the match and earn a title shot at Wrestlemania 19.

Following Royal Rumble, Lesnar's next "feud" was with WWE champion Kurt Angle. Lesnar had helped Angle, who was also represented by Heyman, win the title.

On the *Here Comes the Pain* DVD, Angle talked about Lesnar.

"A lot of guys in this business will jump to the fact that Brock and I are considered very 'stiff'—very aggressive," Angle said. "It's hard to take that out of somebody, you can't take that killer instinct out of anyone that's been doing it for 20 years, because when it comes down to it, if there was ever a fight, we're going to end up on top. We're going to kick some ass and take some names, we have killer instincts. So we're going to be stiff, when you wrestle us you know you're going to wrestle us, because you're going to feel it, and I can't take that out of me. I'm a shooter, I'm a wrestler, I bring that to the table. Brock Lesnar is a shooter, he's a wrestler, he's a 300-pound monster, 6'3", can bench the world, can squat the world, and here he is, you're not going to take that killer instinct out of him. So you know what? When you go out there and you wrestle him, you better be ready and you better be prepared to possibly get injured, although we're in 'entertainment.' But that's what

Brock Lesnar brings to the table, he's real and people need to watch out for him."

On the February 1 live event, Lesnar was scheduled to wrestle RAW world champion Triple H, but Triple H (who was known as Hunter Hearst-Helmsley when he joined WWE) was injured. Instead, Lesnar wrestled and defeated Team Angle (made up of Charlie Haas and Lesnar's former tag-team partner Shelton Benjamin) and then defeated Kurt Angle.

On the February 20 Smackdown, Lesnar defeated Haas and then Benjamin to earn a match with Angle. Lesnar defeated Angle by DQ when Haas and Benjamin entered the ring and attacked Lesnar. Edge and Chris Benoit rescued Lesnar.

Three days later, on the No Way Out pay-per-view event, Lesnar and Benoit defeated Angle and Team Angle in a handicap match. On the February 27 Smackdown, Lesnar defeated Team Angle and then announced he would face Heyman the following week in a steel-cage match. The next week, Lesnar defeated Heyman despite interference from Angle and Team Angle.

But on the next Smackdown, Kurt Angle defeated Lesnar to retain his WWE title.

Two nights after the loss to Angle, in a house show, The Rock and Lesnar wrestled for the first time since the previous SummerSlam. The Rock won the rematch.

Over the next weeks, the feud between Angle and Lesnar heated up. On the March 20 Smackdown, Angle broke a crutch over Lesnar's back. A week later, Angle broke a 2x4 over Lesnar's back. Those incidents set the stage for Wrestlemania 19 on March 30.

The bout, won by Lesnar, would be remembered for its ending. Near the end of the match, Lesnar tried a Shooting Star Press, a move he had completed successfully in the OVW, but this time he did not pull it off correctly. Lesnar's head slammed into Angle's ribcage leaving both wrestlers stunned. Lesnar managed to recover and finish the match.

He defeated Angle to claim the WWE title. Lesnar spent the night in the hospital with a concussion.

In an interview with Get in the Ring radio a few months later, Angle recalled the match's ending. Angle said Lesnar messed up the move because "He lost his balance and was tired. As soon as he landed, [I] thought the two of us were going to be hanging out in the hospital together later that night."

Angle said he "improvised" by immediately covering Brock, and the first thing he thought was that he was going to end up WWE champion for another nine months, but then, "Brock kicked out, and I told him do his thing [the F–5]. Brock was able to do it and that was that."

In an another interview with Off the Record on TSN in Canada, Angle said going into the match that all he could think was that he "was 20 percent and just needed to survive." Angle, who suffered a severe neck injury at the 1996 Olympic Trials, would have neck surgery three times in the 15 months following the match with Lesnar.

Despite the concussion, Lesnar didn't miss much wrestling.

On the April 10 Smackdown, Lesnar defeated John Hardy in a non-title match. The following week, he defeated A-Train after being attacked by John Cena. The next week on Backlash, Lesnar defeated Cena to retain the WWE title.

On the July 27 Vengeance pay-per-view from Denver, Angle reclaimed the WWE title when he defeated Lesnar and the Big Show in a triple-threat match.

In early August, Lesnar was turned into a "heel." On August 24 at SummerSlam in Phoenix, Angle defeated Lesnar to retain the WWE title. Ten days later on Smackdown, McMahon announced that Angle and Lesnar would hold a one-hour iron match for the WWE title.

In mid-August, the WWE released the *Here Comes the Pain* DVD. Several WWE employers talked about what a star Lesnar had become.

Manager Paul Heyman said, "He's the Tiger Woods of this business. He's the Michael Jordan of this business. He's that dominating, he's that much better, he has no peers."

Wrestler Booker T said, "He's caught onto the game, as far as the psychology part of it, faster than anybody I've ever seen. When you see him walk out of that curtain, he's as freaky as anybody you ever want to see. But then, on the other hand, he goes out in the middle of the ring and he can soar and fly like a 180-pound guy, that sets him apart from most guys that I've seen in the business."

Wrestler John Cena said, "He is one of the best pure athletes I've ever seen. I think Brock Lesnar is the future of this company, his potential is unlimited."

Wrestler Brooklyn Brawler said, "Brock Lesnar has broken the barrier from a superstar to a huge superstar."

Wrestler Rey Mysterio said, "We've got a good vibe, we've got a good chemistry together, man. Very focused, very aggressive in the ring, there's nothing like having him on your side."

Two agents summed up Lesnar.

Agent Pat Patterson said, "There's two ways you can take Brock Lesnar, as a wrestler or as a person. He won't bullshit you, he won't lie to you, he's a wonderful person. As a wrestler, he's all business, the guy you see in the ring? That's him, and I'll tell you what, I wouldn't want him to be mad at me."

According to agent Michael Hayes, "He's a monster, he's an educated monster, and there's a difference. He knows when he wants to do something, why he wants to do something, and that's a very dangerous man."

On the September 14 live event, four days before the iron match, Angle and Lesnar had a 40-minute tune-up with Angle winning when Lesnar suffered a knee injury, which appeared serious to some observers. But on the September 18 Smackdown taping in Raleigh, North Carolina, Lesnar defeated Angle to win the WWE championship. On the same show, Eddie Guerrero and Chavo Guerrero defeated Benjamin and Haas to the WWE tag team title.

After defeating Angle, Lesnar's next major opponents were expected by many observers to be the Undertaker, followed by Chris Benoit. But as it was pointed out in the September 22 *Figure Four Weekly* newsletter, "Last year when Brock first won the belt, the plan was for Lesnar to hold it through Wrestlemania 2003, beat Kurt [Angle] there, then go on to lose the belt to Benoit via crossface submission shortly thereafter. As noted a million times before in these pages, plans change. There is a slim possibility that Lesnar could drop the title to the Undertaker at the next PPV because of his injury, but he's been working through serious injuries all this past year [including a very painful rib problem], so...the chances of him taking off are slim unless his knee gets to the point where he's completely immobile."

Despite the knee injury, Lesnar didn't miss any action. In its issue the next week, *Figure Four Weekly* gave an update on Lesnar's knee injury. "The latest on Brock is that he likely has floating cartilage in his knee and will need a scope at some point, so it doesn't look like a torn ACL or MCL as was initially feared."

In the same issue, the newsletter mentioned an interview Lesnar had done the previous week with a Philadelphia radio station. Lesnar was promoting an upcoming house show in Philadelphia. One highlight of the interview was when Lesnar talked about his match with Angle at Wrestlemania. Lesnar conceded the Shooting Star Press was something he "shouldn't have tried." But he added that he might "try it again someday."

On September 27, Smackdown was in Winnipeg, Manitoba. A crowd estimated at 5,000 saw Lesnar defeat Angle with an F–5 to retain the WWE title. The next night, 130 miles west of Winnipeg in Brandon, Manitoba, a patron was escorted out of the arena after slapping Lesnar on the back. Lesnar reportedly shoved back.

In October, Lesnar and the WWE visited Finland, Germany, and England. In Cologne, Germany, Angle and the Undertaker defeated Lesnar and Cena when the Undertaker pinned Lesnar. The next night in Birmingham, England, Lesnar defeated the Undertaker in the main event. The two would meet again the next week with Lesnar defeating the Undertaker in a biker chain match on the No Mercy pay-per-view.

Figure Four Weekly reported in its October 27 newsletter that it appeared that Benoit was in line for Lesnar's title. "One of the original plans was for him to go through Albert and Big Show on successive PPVs before moving on to Brock, but the house show lineups for the next few months indicate he may skip past the Big Show feud."

On the October 27 Smackdown in Augusta, Georgia, Lesnar defeated the 5'11", 229-pound Benoit in the main event. It was announced that the two would be the main event in a house show in Portland, Oregon, on November 23.

In early November, Steve Austin was on the *Howard Stern Show* to promote his new book, *The Stone Cold Truth. Figure Four Weekly* reported that Austin talked about a disagreement with Vince McMahon, who "wanted Austin to lose to Brock in a King of the Ring qualifying match." Austin told McMahon, "No."

The newsletter reported that around the same time as Austin's interview with Stern, Angle did an interview with a San Francisco radio station where he was asked about steroids. His reply, according to the newsletter, was that steroids were not a problem in pro wrestling because it was not an actual athletic contest. He said wrestling was more like a circus. He added there "was no reason to take anything to get a competitive advantage." Angle also said, "Brock was 100 percent natural," and that it was "actually really easy to stay clean."

In mid-November, the Survivor Series PPV was headlined by Team Lesnar against Team Angle in a 10-man elimination match, won by Team Angle. After Lesnar defeated Cena with the F–5 at the Staples Center in Los Angeles on November 22, Team Lesnar won the 20-man Battle Royal on the November 27 Smackdown.

In early December the crew was in South Korea and Australia, with Lesnar beating Benoit in both main events. On the December 4

Smackdown, Lesnar again defeated Benoit for the WWE title. A week later on Smackdown, Heyman announced he was going to "build Smackdown on the back of Brock Lesnar."

In late December, while the company was on a break for the holidays, Lesnar reportedly underwent arthroscopic surgery on his knee and elbow. He returned to action in early January.

In a December interview in *The Straits Times* newspaper in Singapore, Lesnar was asked what he would be doing if he wasn't wrestling. His response was, "Probably playing football. Either that or fighting in an organization like Ultimate Fighting Championship."

As Royal Rumble neared (January 25 in Philadelphia), wrestling observers were talking about WWE's apparent plan for a match featuring Lesnar vs. Goldberg, who had played four years in the NFL before joining the WWE in 1997, at the upcoming Wrestlemania XX (March 14). That match was expected to be the final match with the company for the 6'4", 285-pound Goldberg.

In the issue of *Flex* magazine, which reached newsstands on January 6, 2004, Lesnar was pictured on the cover—believed to be just the second time a pro wrestler had been featured on the magazine's cover.

At the Royal Rumble, Lesnar defeated Hardcore Holly to retain the WWE title. On the same program, Eddie Guerrero won his match to earn a shot at Lesnar on the next pay-per-view.

On February 1 (Super Bowl Sunday), the Smackdown lineup was in Pittsburgh. Before a small crowd, Lesnar defeated hometown hero Kurt Angle and Guerrero to retain the title. From Pittsburgh, the crew went to Regina, Saskatchewan, and Vancouver, British Columbia. Also in February, Lesnar purchased an airplane to use for his WWE travel.

On the February 15 No Way Out pay-per-view, which was taped at the Cow Palace in San Francisco, Guerrero defeated Lesnar—with some help from Goldberg—to win the WWE title.

After the match, Guerrero wrote on the WWE's website, "It's unbelievable. Who'd ever expect a Chicano, 5'9", 220 pounds to win the WWE championship?"

There would soon be more surprises involving Lesnar.

Following the Smackdown taping in Atlantic City, New Jersey, on March 9, Lesnar reportedly told the crew that he was leaving the company following Wrestlemania the next week, to pursue a football career.

Figure Four Weekly reported that during the preceding months, Lesnar had become stressed about the physical and mental demands of the business. He had recently purchased his own airplane to ease the travel demands. He told the Smackdown crew that he could no longer take the stress of the business, that it wasn't fun anymore, and that he wouldn't be coming back.

Figure Four Weekly said, "While most outside of wrestling initially assumed it must be some story that was floated out there to put the result of the [upcoming] Brock vs. Goldberg match in question [since 'everyone knew' that Goldberg, whose contract expired at Mania, was doing the job], those inside the company for the most part believed it to be real."

In its Wrestlemania XX preview, *Figure Four Weekly* said, "Goldberg hasn't re-signed a new deal yet, so the chances of him winning this one are about zero. Stranger things have happened, and it should be noted that Brock has been very unhappy lately because he was told the plans down the road were for the Undertaker to destroy him to get his new [old] persona over again. This is one of those matches that most people would say doesn't look good on paper, however, I think it will be the big surprise of the show. Brock is the best big man ever in wrestling, and Goldberg is way better than a lot of people give him credit for being. I think he'll be a professional here—even though it's his last match with the company—and try to put on a great show, so this could end up being the sleeper match of the evening. Expect an Austin stunner on

Goldberg to cap it all off."

On March 14, Wrestlemania XX was held at Madison Square Garden in New York City. With Stone Cold Steve Austin as a guest referee, Goldberg defeated Lesnar. After the match, Austin went after both Goldberg and Lesnar. Austin gave Lesnar a sendoff with his trademark "Stone Cold Stunner."

Several days after the event, Alex Marvez wrote in the *Fort Lauderdale (Florida) Sun-Sentinel* that "Word of Lesnar's departure leaked before Sunday's Wrestlemania XX match against Bill Goldberg, resulting in a brutal crowd reaction for both in their last scheduled WWE performances. Fans at New York City's Madison Square Garden taunted Lesnar and Goldberg and even started a chant for Hulk Hogan, who wasn't at Wrestlemania XX because of last summer's real-life falling out with WWE owner Vince McMahon."

A week after Wrestlemania, the WWE officially announced Lesnar's departure with this statement on its website, "Brock has wrestled his entire professional career in the WWE, and we are proud of his accomplishments and wish him the best in his new endeavor."

Figure Four Weekly recapped Lesnar's WWE career. "Two years ago, he was called up to the main roster with the idea that he would be pushed straight toward the WWE title. While he wasn't ready for the big time on day one, he was within a matter of months as he picked up things extraordinarily quickly after being put in the ring with several great workers.

"At SummerSlam that year, he beat The Rock clean for the title, and the company seemed primed to take around him. By the time 2004 rolled around, Lesnar had been on top for two years and had become quite possibly the best big man ever in the history of wrestling. However, things were changing. Around January, he was informed that the Undertaker would be returning as the Dead Man, and that one of his first feuds would be with Lesnar. The two had feuded shortly after Lesnar first won the belt, and while he finally got a clean pin in a cage match at the end, the feud did Lesnar no favors. In this instance, he wasn't getting a clean win in the end.

"Worse, every time he'd ever lost the title in the past, the plans were for him to get it back at some point. This time he was being moved away from Eddie Guerrero, and there were no plans to put the title back on him. All of this, combined with the stress of the road and the fact that he's been in constant pain for at least a year [he never took time off to heal any of his chronic injuries, which included screwed up knees, ribs, neck, etc.] caused him to throw in the towel."

Within a month of Wrestlemania XX, Austin, Goldberg, and Lesnar all left the WWE. Lesnar was walking away from a contract, which was to pay him—depending on the report—anywhere from $10 million to $45 million over seven years. The $10 million figure was probably closer to the real amount.

Marvez wrote, "Lesnar's departure was a major blow to a Smackdown roster already reeling from the news that Kurt Angle is again out of action indefinitely because of another neck-related injury. But in the long run, Lesnar's departure could become a positive if he decides to return. By hyping the fact he turned his back on wrestling fans, Lesnar has the potential to become the industry's top villain again."

Lesnar explained his decision in an interview with Minneapolis radio station KFAN. Lesnar told the station he'd "grown up always wanting to play in the NFL," and while "his last three years with the WWE were great," he'd grown unhappy with it.

He said his decision wasn't about money, it was about "being happy" and that he didn't want to be 40 years old looking back and wondering why he "didn't at least try."

Lesnar said he informed McMahon of his decision two weeks before Wrestlemania and said he was "flat-out tired from all the travel."

He conceded that buying his own airplane "was an attempt to mask the problems, and it failed." He said if he didn't make an NFL team, he would have no interest in the CFL or NFL Europe. Asked if he'd wrestle again someday, he said, "I'm walking away from the wrestling business for now."

Earlier in the interview he said, "I'm not saying I may never go back there someday."

In an interview with *Maxim* magazine in the spring of 2009, Lesnar recalled the Survivor Series in November 2002 when he wrestled despite injuries.

"I had three broken ribs and a bad knee," Lesnar said. "During that period, I would take a couple of Vicodin and wash 'em down with a few slugs of vodka. That's what got me through. The ribs didn't heal for another eight months because there's no off-season in pro wrestling. We were in New Jersey, I believe. I can't even remember where I was hardly."

Lesnar admitted in the magazine interview that he owed his fame to his WWE career but, "You get so brainwashed. You're on the road 300 days a year, and that's why guys get so messed up. This life becomes a part of them. It's not real, but some guys who are still in the business think that it is. You look at Mickey Rourke in [the 2008 movie] *The Wrestler*—he just couldn't let it go. You live a double life. I was tired of trying to be who I was in the ring and then coming home for two days to be normal. They didn't allow you to be. The guys who get out are the smart ones, really and truly."

Ironically, after his departure from the WWE, he was featured in the April issue of *Smackdown* magazine. He also appeared in the latest issue of *Flex* magazine in an ad for a supplement, which he said he used so he could stay "on top of the WWE for years to come."

In mid-April, Goldberg did a chat on AOL. Talking about Lesnar, Goldberg said he was "all for guys pursuing their dreams, so more power to him." Goldberg said he wasn't totally against returning to the WWE at some point.

In late April, Austin also left the WWE. In a statement on its website, the WWE announced, "After months of negotiations, the WWE and

Steve Austin have been unable to come to terms on a new contract and as a result have mutually agreed to part company. Both parties have left the door open to work together again in the future, and the WWE wishes Steve the very best in his future endeavors."

The disagreement between Austin and the WWE was over Austin wanting the rights to the name "Stone Cold Steve Austin" for his business purposes outside of the WWE.

In late April, Chris Benoit did an interview with Off the Record on TSN in Canada. Benoit said he respected Lesnar's decision to leave WWE, but because Lesnar was "a wrestler" and had done it for so long, "someday he would be back."

DAVE MELTZER

At an early age, Dave Meltzer showed an interest in professional wrestling. By the time he was 21, Meltzer had turned that interest into a source of income.

Meltzer started the *Wrestling Observer Newsletter* to keep readers informed about pro wrestling from regions other than the region they lived in. Within five years, Meltzer resigned his job as a sports writer at a daily newspaper in California to devote his full-time attention to the newsletter.

Meltzer built the newsletter into the bible of the professional wrestling industry. The newsletter is now available by subscription online at F4Wonline.com. Meltzer also serves as co-host, along with Bryan Alvarez, the editor of *Figure Four Weekly* newsletter, on a weekly radio show.

In 2007, *Sports Illustrated* senior writer Frank Deford wrote that "Meltzer, I believe, is the most accomplished reporter in sports journalism." Deford praised Meltzer for his work documenting the death toll in the sport of professional wrestling.

In addition to covering professional wrestling, Meltzer, who lives in San Jose, California, has covered MMA and UFC fights extensively and has served as a UFC judge.

Meltzer has followed Brock Lesnar closely since Lesnar joined Ohio Valley Wrestling in 2000. "When Brock came up [to the WWF] in 2001, he was brought [up] before his trainers thought he was ready," Meltzer said. "But he had this lucrative contract and the company rushed him.

"But he became a star within a couple of weeks. By August he was a star in a match with The Rock. It doesn't take 18 months to create a star in the WWE [as boss Vince McMahon has said on occasion]. It only takes a month if you do it right and have all the muscle behind you. With Brock, 90 percent of it was muscle, and he became a star quickly."

At the beginning of his professional wrestling career, observers thought that former University of Minnesota heavyweight Shelton Benjamin, who was Lesnar's tag-team partner in Ohio Valley Wrestling, would become a star in the WWE before Lesnar did.

"Shelton probably picked up wrestling quicker than Brock," Meltzer said. "But he didn't have Lesnar's backing. They had so much invested in Brock. The WWE had found Shelton when they were scouting Brock. But they gave Shelton a lot less money than Brock. Most wrestlers will tell you that Shelton should have been a superstar, but the company never got behind him."

Benjamin went on to have a 10-year career in the WWE. Lesnar became more than just one of pro wrestling's stars he became one of the best heavyweights in the history of pro wrestling. But less than two years after winning the WWE heavyweight championship, Lesnar left the WWE.

"When I first heard about his departure from WWE, I was surprised because he had done well," Meltzer said. "But in hindsight, I shouldn't have been."

After winning the WWE title for the first time, it appeared Lesnar would be one of the promotion's featured stars. He lost the title twice and won it back both times.

"At first, it looked like the company would build around him," Meltzer said. "When he lost, you knew that he would win it back. But the company phased him out. When he lost the title to Eddie [Guerrero], Brock was not the guy anymore. They did kind of give up on him. Maybe not give up, but they did move him down."

Meltzer said there were signs of Lesnar's growing dissatisfaction with the business.

"In hindsight, long before that, you could see that the road and the lifestyle were not good for Brock," Meltzer said. "He told me one time that he had looked around the locker room, at all those guys, probably in their late 30s, and saw his future. At the time, it was a surprise, but looking back, pro wrestling was not the best fit for Brock. I think he has to be 100 percent motivated to do well at something. When that [motivation] went away in pro wrestling, he left."

Meltzer, who covers the UFC for Yahoo! Sports, has not been surprised by Lesnar's success in the UFC.

"The [amateur] wrestling background helps a lot," Meltzer said. "But everything is different. To be successful, it's not just being a good amateur wrestler. It's being a high-level athlete in wrestling, jiujitsu, and boxing. If you're good at any of these, you'll have success.

"Brock was so good as a wrestler. But he had some natural ability at MMA and he quickly moved to the top. He got some breaks because he had been a star in the WWE, but he still had to win. They [UFC] handed him a shot at the title, [but] they didn't hand him the title. He didn't have any easy opponents. He's faced the top guys. He asked for that. He easily could have taken another route."

Meltzer said that the UFC is a good fit for Lesnar. "UFC is definitely a sport made for him," Meltzer said. "If he had started UFC right after college, he probably would be better now, because he'd be more experienced. But the timing wasn't good for him [and the UFC] coming out of college. The UFC wasn't as big then [in 2000]. He was five to six years too early for the UFC."

After becoming a star in the WWE, Lesnar also become a star in the UFC, as well. "Top stars are needed in both genres," Meltzer said. "Both sports are more or less the same. But you can be a bigger star in the WWE because the company can control it better, and you can be a star longer. In the UFC it's harder because you have to keep winning."

In the spring of 2010, Meltzer said the upcoming Lesnar–Shane Carwin match would be lucrative for the UFC. "The last one [Lesnar's fight against Frank Mir in July 2009] did 1.6 million Pay-Per-Views," Meltzer said. "This one will do well."

Meltzer said that a match between the top two MMA heavyweights in the world—Lesnar and Russian Fedor Emelianenko—could eventually happen.

"Yes, it's possible," Meltzer said. "It's just a contractual thing. He [Fedor] is under contract to a different organization. But that would be a big fight."

MICHAEL RAND

Minneapolis Star Tribune sports reporter and team leader Michael Rand has covered college wrestling extensively. He was asked what stood out about Brock Lesnar. Rand wrote the following:

The thing that stood out immediately upon seeing Brock Lesnar up close for the first time was the size of his upper body. It was the late 1990s, and Lesnar was emerging onto the NCAA wrestling scene with the University of Minnesota. There are plenty of muscular competitors in a sport that demands incredible self-discipline, but Lesnar was different. His chest, neck, and even head had a thickness that was almost cartoonish—and definitely got people's attention.

"I've seen him walk out onto the mat and you watch the opponent and you see fear in their eyes. He's so top-heavy that he's intimidating,"

Billy Pierce, another former Gophers heavyweight, once told me in regards to Lesnar. "Some of the duals I've seen, the guys are beaten before the dual even starts. Even some of the top-ranked guys, they're beaten before they even go out there."

And Lesnar thrived on it. He once said in an interview with me, "I like the feeling of going out there and humiliating somebody. If you step on the mat with me, it means you think you can beat me, and I like destroying that."

Still, despite a reputation for being a crowd pleaser, there was a contrasting shyness to Lesnar—a reluctance to be too boldly placed in the spotlight. At least that's what I perceived, and it's why I never really thought much of his post-college-wrestling foray into the world of rasslin'.

The good folks at the WWF (later WWE) agreed. Said then-VP for talent relations Bill Ross in a 2001 interview with me, "We know he can deliver the steak. We have to work on his sizzle. Your governor was long on sizzle. He needs to take a page from your governor's book and enhance his charisma. But it's not uncommon at all. And it's not a big concern."

Apparently it wasn't. There aren't a whole lot of career options within one's field for a former college wrestler, but Lesnar certainly ended up making the most of his. When I think back on Lesnar's journey—from college wrestling to WWF/WWE to a brief flirtation with the NFL and the Vikings to his status now in the world of Mixed Martial Arts...well, suffice to say it's a little mind-boggling.

Seriously, who would have ever thought that Lesnar would eventually find so much "sizzle" that he would marry WWE vixen Sable, start a line of clothing called Death Clutch and, well, have books written about him. I'll admit I never saw it coming, even when I first looked a decade ago at the hulking figure at heavyweight who could electrify a college wrestling crowd like few others.

CHAPTER 6

MOVING ON

The physical and mental demands of professional wrestling had taken a toll on Brock Lesnar.

"I wasn't ready for what [McMahon] had put on my plate. I couldn't eat it all," Lesnar told the *Bismarck Tribune*. "I tried to, you know. That's just me being me. He asked me, 'Are you ready for this?' And I just said, 'Bring it on. Let's go.' I wasn't ready to be traveling 300 days a year. I wasn't ready to be a husband. I wasn't ready for a lot of things. I had a lot of growing up to do. I was forced to grow up."

Triple H, in an interview with *Byte This* on the WWE's website in April 2004, talked about Lesnar's departure from WWE. Triple H said if a person couldn't handle the business, then he was "all for them getting out." He said he didn't mean that in a "derogatory" way and that the only thing he didn't like about the situation was that "Brock decided to leave and then just left." He added that he felt Lesnar handled it wrong and predicted that Lesnar would come back to the WWE at some point and that would be sooner than he saw him "playing in a Super Bowl."

The May 3 edition of RAW was taped in Phoenix with Lesnar in attendance. According to lordsofpain.com, Lesnar and McMahon "were able to talk in a very civil manner. While McMahon does not like the way Brock left the company so quickly, he understands that he could return to WWE, at some point, so he doesn't want to burn any bridges between them."

In early June, McMahon did a two-part interview with *Off The Record* on TSN in Canada. McMahon told host Michael Landsberg that the problem with Lesnar, "wasn't that he didn't like the schedule," but that he "wasn't very good around other people." McMahon said that Lesnar was an "introvert" and that was a problem the WWE had with several wrestlers who had come up from amateur wrestling. McMahon said Lesnar's decision to leave was "wild" and "took him by surprise." He added that Lesnar's decision "hurt" the company.

There were plenty of other skeptics who said Lesnar, who hadn't played football since high school in 1995, couldn't make the transition from pro wrestling to pro football.

The skeptics motivated Lesnar.

"People said I wouldn't be any good at amateur wrestling. Well, I won an NCAA title," Lesnar told the *Minneapolis Star Tribune*. "People said I couldn't be a pro wrestler. Well, I was WWE champion twice. Now people say I can't play football…. But I say I can."

Lesnar had begun his workouts in April at a training facility in Tempe, Arizona, with the immediate goal of working out for NFL teams at the facility in May. A workout, which five teams Green Bay, Philadelphia, Kansas City, Dallas, and San Francisco had agreed to attend, was scheduled for May 18.

But the workout had to be postponed. On April 17, Lesnar suffered a broken jaw and left hand, bruised pelvis, and pulled groin muscle in a motorcycle accident. The injuries delayed his training for at least three weeks. The workout was rescheduled for June 2 but had to be postponed again when he aggravated the groin injury. The workout was eventually canceled.

"I ain't afraid of anything, and I ain't afraid of anybody," Lesnar told the *Minneapolis Star Tribune*. "I've been an underdog in athletics since I was five. I got zero college offers for wrestling. Now people say I can't play football, that it's a joke. But I say I can. I'm as good an athlete as guys in the NFL, if not better."

"I ain't afraid of anything, and I ain't afraid of anybody."
—Brock Lesnar

The 6'3", 280-pound Lesnar certainly had numbers that would pique the interest of football coaches—bench press (475 pounds), squat (695 pounds), and a 4.65 in the 40-yard dash.

Indianapolis Colts coach Tony Dungy was intrigued.

"Obviously, he's strong enough, flexible enough, big enough, and has the quick-twitch fiber muscles," Dungy told the *Minneapolis Star Tribune*. "And winning an NCAA heavyweight title is harder than playing defensive line. So who knows? The only question is he's 26. How long will it take for him to learn how to play the game?"

Lesnar convinced the Minnesota Vikings coaching staff to let him work out for the team. After two workouts—one in June and one in July—Lesnar was signed to a one-year contract with the Vikings for the 2004–05 season.

Vikings coach Mike Tice told the *Minneapolis Star Tribune* that Lesnar was "too intriguing" to leave off the Vikings' 83-man training camp roster.

"We have an interest in everybody that can help," Tice said. "But it will be a tough, tough transition for Brock being that he hasn't played much ball.

"Remember, this guy is a world-class athlete. This is no bum we're talking about. Is he raw? Yes, of course he is raw. But what I told him is to be patient. I know I'm going to be patient. A guy like him, you never know. It's worth the effort."

The Vikings, who were the only team to work out Lesnar, hadn't made the playoffs in the previous three seasons.

"I've been given an opportunity to play football in Minnesota," Lesnar told the *Minneapolis Star Tribune*. "I'm so thankful to Mike Tice and this organization. When I got into my motorcycle accident, I didn't know if I would get a fair opportunity. So today is special for me. I'm going to go home, relax, and get ready to go down to Mankato [where the Vikings held the first three weeks of training camp]. I'm just going to go to war, I guess."

Tice told the *Minneapolis Star Tribune* that Lesnar, who would work out at defensive tackle, would be "brought along slowly. We're not going to throw him to the wolves, and we're not going to embarrass him."

In an interview with ESPN around July 4, Lesnar said he "regretted going from college straight to the WWE" and wished he'd gone into football instead. He chose the WWE because he "just wanted to make some money" because he "didn't want to be poor anymore."

From the first day of training camp—July 31—Lesnar showed he was serious about football. Although he wasn't 100 percent physically because of the motorcycle accident, he didn't miss one repetition in practice. And he studied diligently.

From Lesnar's first practice, the Minnesota media provided daily updates on him and his progress.

At 8:15 AM on Saturday, July 31—the first day of practice—Lesnar was on the practice field with defensive assistant Jim Panagos, working on a lineman's three-point stance. The *Minneapolis Star Tribune*'s report on the first practice said Lesnar "was like any other rookie; standing at the back of the line for drills and volunteering for duty on the scout offense."

The next day, Lesnar sat out team drills and got only five repetitions in pass-rushing drills. In those drills, defensive linemen go one-on-one against offensive linemen with a goal of pushing the blocker into a

March 20, 1999: Cal State Bakersfield's Stephen Neal challenges Minnesota's Brock Lesnar in the heavyweight class of the Men's Division I Wrestling Championship held at Pennsylvania State University in State College. Neal defeated Lesnar for the championship title. (Doug Benedict/NCAA Photos. NCAA Photos via AP Images)

March 18, 2000: Minnesota's Brock Lesnar (right) defeated Iowa's Wes Hand (left) in the heavyweight championship match during the NCAA Division I Wrestling Championships held at the Kiel Center in St. Louis, Missouri. *(Marv Butkus/NCAA Photos via AP Images)*

Brock Lesnar takes a break between drills at the Minnesota Vikings Training Camp on August 7, 2004. *(Photo by Tom Dahlin/Getty Images)*

World Wrestling Entertainment wrestler Brock Lesnar attends a media conference at ESPN Zone in Times Square on March 18, 2003, in New York City announcing the All-Star lineup of WWE WrestleMania XIX. *(Photo by Mark Mainz/Getty Images)*

Former WWE star Brock Lesnar, now fighting as a mixed martial arts heavyweight, strikes a pose at the weigh-in for UFC 87 on Friday, August 8, 2008, at the Target Center in Minneapolis, Minnesota. *(AP Photo/Neil Davidson, CP)*

Brock Lesnar (top) punches Randy Couture during their UFC World Heavyweight Mixed Martial Arts championship match on Saturday, November 15, 2008, in Las Vegas. Lesnar won by TKO in the second round. *(AP Photo/Eric Jamison)*

Right: Brock Lesnar (left) and Frank Mir battle for the UFC 100 Heavyweight title on Saturday, July 11, 2009, in Las Vegas at the Mandalay Bay Events Center. *(AP Photo/Alaric Lambert)*

Brock Lesnar celebrates his UFC heavyweight Mixed Martial Arts title match win against Shane Carwin on Saturday, July 3, 2010, at the MGM Grand Garden Arena in Las Vegas. *(AP Photo/Eric Jamison)*

dummy bag or by getting past the blocker and reaching the bag. Lesnar wasn't successful in any of his five repetitions.

Vikings defensive line coach Brian Baker told the *Minneapolis Star Tribune*, "They got the best of Brock today. There wasn't a lot to be positive about, other than he kept working. He's got a champion's heart."

Baker added that Lesnar was progressing at the rate he expected—"slowly"—and that he hoped to have Lesnar ready to participate in team drills within two or three days.

Lesnar told the *Minneapolis Star Tribune* he wasn't discouraged. "I'm having fun. It's my first day of contact. I have a lot to learn."

The next day August 2, Lesnar made his debut in team drills. Because of the warm temperatures and high humidity in Mankato, Vikings coach Mike Tice wanted all 12 defensive linemen to share equally in the drills, and he had Lesnar split time with rookie Spencer Johnson.

About 45 minutes into the first drill, Lesnar made his first tackle.

Tice told the *Minneapolis Star Tribune*, "He grew up some. We were pleased. He's been working hard, and I thought it was important for him to get a little taste today and see what it's like. I'm sure that his head is spinning some, but he was able to make a tackle."

The next day, after competing in team drills for the second consecutive day, Lesnar told the *Minneapolis Star Tribune*, "Sometimes little things are discouraging, but I've got to remember that this is my fourth day in a professional football camp. I think I'm doing okay. I'm not setting expectations for myself. I just want to learn something here every day and take it one day at a time."

The newspaper's critique of Lesnar's performance through four days of practice said he was "still looking like someone who hasn't played football since high school. He's slow off the ball and needs to get better penetration in order to have an impact."

The fifth day of practice saw Lesnar make progress in the pass-rushing drill, in which he had been shut out the three previous days. In his first try, going against offensive lineman Adam Haayer, he failed, and on his second attempt he jumped before the ball was snapped. But on the third attempt, he succeeded. Going against Haayer again, Lesnar was able to get past Haayer and tip over the blocking dummy.

One interested onlooker noting Lesnar's performance at practice was another professional wrestling star—Sable. Five days later, on August 10, World Wrestling Entertainment's website announced that Sable, whose real name was Rena Mero, had left the organization "to spend more time with her family."

Two days later, things got interesting for Lesnar and the Vikings.

Day 7 of training camp in Mankato was scheduled to feature two practices between the Vikings and the Kansas City Chiefs. The Chiefs had made the 115-mile trip from their training camp in River Falls, Wisconsin. A year earlier, the Vikings had traveled to River Falls and the practices were interrupted by a brawl between the teams. To avoid a repeat, Tice and Chiefs coach Dick Vermiel agreed to "minor contact."

The agreement didn't have much effect. The morning practice session between the teams was punctuated by two full-squad brawls and several other smaller skirmishes. The evening practice, in front of an estimated 6,000 fans, saw two more brawls after the Chiefs applied late hits to Vikings running backs. Lesnar may have been one reason for the late hits.

Lesnar had ignored a no-contact rule for quarterbacks and hit Chiefs quarterback Damon Huard. Lesnar, who had got past Chiefs guard Jonathon Ingram, drilled his helmet into Huard's stomach. Huard had to go to the sideline to catch his breath.

A little later, Lesnar tackled Chiefs running back Jonathan Smith. Ingram then shoved Lesnar, who responded by jumping on Ingram's back. Lesnar and Ingram were joined by players from both teams.

"That's just me, and I don't care what the Chiefs think about it," Lesnar told the *Minneapolis Star Tribune*. "I'm here to play football and make the team. I'm going 110 percent. I'm not going to dial it down.

That's the game. We've got full pads on. If that's the tempo they want to play, maybe my tempo is a little different.

"I've got to prove myself. If it's fighting and clawing and whatever, then that's what I'm going to do. I haven't had this much fun since...I can't remember. I have only one speed. Sometimes I got too far past the line and had to come back. I've got to find that happy medium, and I don't know if I've got it. But at least I'm getting up there and causing some chaos."

The newspaper reported that Tice "barely suppressed a grin when asked about Lesnar."

"He's still a little lost at times," Tice said. "But he's not going to back down from anyone. He's going to give extreme effort. We're really pleased to have him around. He's good for the team."

The Chiefs and Vikings went through some more 11-on-11 drills the next day. It was much quieter than the previous day until the final play of the practice. Lesnar and Chiefs tackle Kevin Sampson got locked up and fell to the ground. They came up pushing each other before being separated.

On August 14 at the Metrodome in Minneapolis—twelve days after their first practice with full pads—the Vikings opened their four-game preseason schedule. Aside from Lesnar, the game provided Vikings fans another interesting angle—the return of former Vikings coach Dennis Green, who was the coach of the Arizona Cardinals.

Lesnar made his Vikings debut in the first half. The Vikings took a 10–3 lead on a 30-yard field goal by Aaron Elling with 8:45 remaining in the first half. On the ensuing kickoff, Lesnar lined up as part of the kickoff team. Lesnar sprinted down the field and hit the Cardinals' blocking wedge, helping to stop the Cardinals' return at their 28-yard line.

After the Vikings scored to take a 23–6 lead with 6:36 remaining in the game, Lesnar made his debut at defensive tackle. The Cardinals needed just two plays (gains of 16 and 32 yards) to move down the field to a first down at the Vikings' 17-yard line. The Cardinals' drive stalled in part because of Lesnar. On first down, Cardinals rookie Nick Leckey was called for offensive holding against Lesnar. The 10-yard penalty wiped out a 6-yard gain and pushed the Cardinals back to the 27. They eventually missed a 44-yard field goal.

After the game, Lesnar told the *Minneapolis Star Tribune*, "This is all I can ask for, to get a little experience. I've been in the league what? Two weeks. I'm just fortunate to have gotten in the game tonight."

On August 18, the Vikings concluded the Mankato portion of their training camp, and on August 20, they played their second exhibition.

In that game, the Vikings built a 17–0 lead early in the second quarter, but the host Atlanta Falcons rallied for a 27–24 victory.

The Falcons pulled within 17–13 at halftime, but the Vikings scored early in the third quarter to take a 24–13 lead. The Falcons narrowed the Vikings' lead to 24–20 going into the fourth quarter and scored with 6:47 remaining to take the lead. The Falcons had rallied behind backup quarterback Matt Schaub, who passed for 205 yards and three touchdowns.

Lesnar saw limited action—just three plays.

The Vikings went into their third exhibition—against the San Francisco 49ers at the Metrodome on Friday, August 27—with their first roster cuts looming. By August 31, the Vikings needed to cut at least 13 players.

Lesnar conceded that he probably wouldn't survive the first cut but was hopeful of making the eight-player practice squad.

"My body's not real good right now," Lesnar told the *Minneapolis Star Tribune* two days before the 49ers game, "but what the heck. For now, I'm living the NFL experience. Who else like me did what I did this summer?"

The Vikings built a 16–0 lead in the first half against the 49ers. After the 49ers pulled within 16–10 early in the fourth quarter, the Vikings scored again to take a 23–10 lead.

The 49ers took over at their own 12-yard line with 22 seconds remaining in the game. On the final play of the game, the 49ers' Jason Wright gained five yards before being tackled by Lesnar.

Three days later, Lesnar was cut by the Vikings.

Tice told the *Minneapolis Star Tribune* that he told Lesnar that he should consider playing in NFL Europe the following spring. Tice said the Vikings would consider re-signing Lesnar in the spring and allocating him to NFL Europe.

"We'd be proud to have him be a Viking and representing us in NFL Europe and continue his development," Tice said. "That's a perfect venue for a guy like Brock Lesnar."

While he couldn't overcome his nine-year layoff from football, Lesnar did earn the respect of the Vikings coaching staff and the players.

Vikings defensive line coach Brian Baker told the *Minneapolis Star Tribune*, "I definitely was upset at first [when the Vikings signed Lesnar], but the thing about Brock is he flat-out earned my respect the past four weeks. I don't know how else to put it."

Baker added that Lesnar "hasn't attempted one shortcut. He sits in the front of the defensive line meeting room. He works on fundamentals with defensive assistant Jim Panagos for 45 minutes before and after most practices. He takes criticism very well. And probably most important, he didn't miss a single rep.

"Initially, I didn't understand why we signed him, and I was mad that we cut a young rookie player [Jeff Womble of Florida State] who at least knew how to play football. But Brock earned it. You could pick 1,000 guys in his situation and not one of them would have lasted this long."

Minneapolis Star Tribune reporter Mark Craig wrote that Baker's thoughts were the consensus of the coaching staff and players.

"I thought we would have been the last team in the world to sign him," offensive guard Chris Liwienski told Craig. "And then they signed him and we all kind of went, 'Oh my gosh. What's this guy going to be all about? Is he going to come in here and tie me in a knot?' But Brock came to work, and guys took notice."

Center Matt Birk agreed. "Brock didn't come in here thinking he was a big shot. He took it seriously and kept his mouth shut."

Linebacker Chris Claiborne summed the situation up, "All I know is the guy turned out to be real cool."

Tice told the *Minneapolis Star Tribune*, "I think at some point this season you'll see Brock Lesnar back, unless another team signs him."

Tice added that he thought Lesnar would be a "really good inside nickel pass rusher one day."

A week after the Vikings cut Lesnar, the Winnipeg Blue Bombers of the Canadian Football League placed Lesnar on their negotiation list. This meant that if Lesnar decided to play in Canada, the Blue Bombers controlled his exclusive rights.

Ed Hitchcock, Lesnar's agent, told the *Minneapolis Star Tribune* that Lesnar still hoped "to land a spot on an NFL practice squad."

But no NFL teams were intrigued enough to sign Lesnar to either their practice squad or sign him and have him play in NFL Europe, which was a developmental league that played in the spring.

"The only regret I would ever have is not doing something," Lesnar told the *Bismarck Tribune* in 2005. "I can tell my grandkids and my kids—I mean, I might not have made the team. But how many kids from Webster, South Dakota, have got a football card in a Minnesota Vikings jersey? I'm man enough to admit that I wasn't ready for that either, but I just threw myself in there. There's only one way I know, and that's full throttle and to the wolves."

CHAPTER 7

TRANSITIONS

In late November 2004, Shelton Benjamin, Lesnar's former OVW tag team partner, did an interview with *The Sun* of London, England. Benjamin told the newspaper he still didn't understand why Lesnar had left WWE.

"I'd have killed for his position," Benjamin said in the interview, "and there was no way things could get any better for him. I saw Brock as possibly being the next Hogan, and if that didn't make him happy, then it was probably best that he moved on. But if he finds it in his heart to come back, then I would welcome him with open arms."

In late December, the *Minneapolis Star Tribune* reported that "friends of former Gopher and pro wrestler Brock Lesnar say he is ready to make a comeback."

That item immediately fueled speculation on the Internet that Lesnar would soon return to the WWE. The speculation increased in early January when Lesnar appeared as a front-row guest at a New Japan Wrestling show at the Tokyo Dome. Promoter Antonio Inoki said Lesnar was the "hottest freelancer in the world" and that Lesnar was interested in joining New Japan, K–1, or PRIDE. While in Japan, Lesnar announced that he and Rena Mero would be getting married.

According to *Figure Four Weekly*, in late January 2005 New Japan was hinting that Lesnar would get a shot at the IWGP heavyweight title at a show at the Tokyo Dome in May.

But before Lesnar could compete in Japan, there was a legal issue.

When Lesnar left the WWE in March 2004, he signed a no-compete clause. In February 2005, with no football teams showing any interest, Lesnar filed a lawsuit against the WWE in U.S. District Court in Connecticut. According to the *Minneapolis Star Tribune*, the lawsuit said the no-compete clause was too vague and "unenforceable."

According to court documents cited in the *Minneapolis Star Tribune*, the agreement restricted Lesnar from working "in the business of professional wrestling, ultimate fighting, and/or sports entertainment in any capacity whatsoever through June 30, 2010."

David Olson, a Minneapolis attorney representing Lesnar, told the newspaper, "Basically, Brock needs to go back to work. Wrestling and contact sports are what he knows."

Hitchcock, Lesnar's agent, told the newspaper that his client "still wants to play football."

In April, in its response to Lesnar's lawsuit, the WWE responded by suing Lesnar. The WWE asked the court to "prohibit him from working as a wrestler or ultimate fighter anywhere in the world."

The company claimed that Lesnar's lawsuit was an attempt to sue his way back into the company. According to *Figure Four Weekly*, the WWE's argument was that Lesnar left the company and now wanted a deal better than the seven-year deal he signed in 2003. The company "rejected Lesnar's unreasonable offers."

The company also claimed that if Lesnar worked for any other "non-WWE sports entertainment company in the world before 2010," it would cause the company "irreparable harm." The WWE also argued that Lesnar's appearance at the New Japan show in Tokyo in January was a breach of the "settlement agreement" between the two when the company "allowed" Lesnar to try out for the NFL.

While in Bismarck in June 2005 for his induction into the Bismarck State College Hall of Fame, Lesnar talked to the *Bismarck Tribune* about the lawsuit. "I'm ready for it [settlement] now. With the lawsuit and everything going on, I just hope we can resolve this thing, and Vince can open his doors to me and just give me a second chance. I have no idea [where it stands]. I guess it stands on the end of your pencil, when it gets on the Internet. That's probably where he'll catch the news. It's either that or me calling him. But I don't know what else I'd be. What else is there for me?"

Lesnar was asked if he would consider coaching.

"I love coaching," Lesnar told the newspaper. "I think I would make an excellent coach. My heart was there for that, but the timing isn't. I don't think I could commit right now to it, because I know that there's other carrots out there dangling in front of me."

"I think I would make an excellent coach."
—Brock Lesnar

In July, Lesnar and the WWE reportedly dropped their claims against each other and begin negotiations that would lead to Lesnar's return to the WWE. The company reported on its website that company officials had met with Lesnar. The report quoted Lesnar, "I don't know if I'm returning to the WWE. I really don't. In order for this to happen, it has to work for both Vince and myself."

In the last week of July, a report on the WWE website said that Lesnar's attorneys were looking over a new contract offer. A week later, on August 2, the website reported, "After verbally agreeing to terms with WWE, Brock Lesnar has decided to withdraw from any involvement with the company."

Jim Ross wrote in his weekly report on the WWE's website, "In my personal opinion, Brock Lesnar is making a big mistake by not accepting WWE's very fair contract offer."

On September 13, it was announced in Japan that Lesnar would compete in a New Japan show in Tokyo on October 8. Eight days after the announcement, the lawsuit between Lesnar and WWE entered into settlement. But the settlement talks broke down again.

Figure Four Weekly said that the WWE gave Lesnar "a low-ball offer" when he went "groveling back." The newsletter also said the WWE's case against Lesnar was weak because earlier in the year, when the WWE downsized by releasing about 20 wrestlers, none of them were prohibited from working in Japan.

But on October 8, in a pay-per-view event from the Tokyo Dome, Lesnar defeated Kazuyuki Fujita and Masa Chono to win the IWGP heavyweight title. Fujita had been the reigning champion. Chono had won New Japan's G–1 title earlier in the year.

Later that month, Total Nonstop Action Wrestling (TNA) promoter Jeff Jarrett was interviewed by *The Sun* in London. After saying he was "re-inventing" wrestling, he was asked if he was negotiating with free agents like Chris Jericho, Lesnar, or Sting.

According to *Figure Four Weekly*, Jarrett's response to the question was interesting for what he didn't say. "To my knowledge, Jericho is not available. But if we're having negotiations with stars, it's in our best interests to keep them under wraps."

The newsletter said, "Make no mistake, they want Brock. Brock works for New Japan, and they obviously have some sort of relationship with New Japan. Whether they can actually get [Lesnar] depends on what sort of settlement he got from WWE."

In early November it was announced in Japan that Lesnar would defend his IWGP title in a singles match against Fujita on January 4, 2006, at the Tokyo Dome.

In mid-November, the pro wrestling business got bad news. Eddie

Guerrero, who had defeated Lesnar on the No Way Out pay-per-view to claim the WWE title, died on November 13. Guerrero, who was 38, was found in his hotel room in downtown Minneapolis. An autopsy revealed that his death was due to heart failure and cardiovascular disease.

After failing to reach a settlement agreement with Lesnar, the WWE went back to court on December 6 to ask for a temporary restraining order to prevent Lesnar from working several upcoming New Japan house shows and the Tokyo Dome Show on January 4.

In response to the WWE's filing, Lesnar's lawyer noted how the WWE delayed settlement for months and also noted that just as Lesnar was set to go to work, the company wanted to prevent him from working.

Less than a week later, Lesnar worked two house shows on December 10 and December 11 and defended his IWGP title with victories over Manabu Nakanishi and Yuji Nagata.

On December 30, the WWE withdrew its request for the temporary restraining order to stop Lesnar from appearing in Tokyo on January 4. On that night in front of an estimated Tokyo Dome crowd of 40,000, Lesnar defeated Shinsuke Nakamura, who had replaced Fujita on the card, to retain the IWGP title.

Ten days after the event in Tokyo, a judge told the WWE that unless it presented a good argument before January 25, he would issue a summary judgment for Lesnar, allowing him to work anywhere. But on January 25, the court granted the WWE a two-week delay until February 8 to present its case.

Finally on April 24, the WWE announced on its website that the two sides had settled their lawsuits. Terms of the settlement were not announced, but Olson told the *Minneapolis Star Tribune* that the settlement would allow Lesnar to "pursue new ventures while he is still in his athletic prime."

The WWE issued a statement saying it was "pleased with the deal" and "believes that the settlement agreement appropriately protects WWE's substantial investment in Brock Lesnar's wrestling character."

It was believed that the agreement allowed Lesnar to go to work for any Mixed Martial Arts company in the world or any pro wrestling company outside of the United States, which would prevent Lesnar from working for Jarrett and TNA.

Olson said that Lesnar "was considering a variety of career options, including mixed martial arts competition, movies, and television." He added that Lesnar was "not considering a WWE return."

In a radio interview shortly after the agreement was announced, Lesnar hinted at the possibility of joining the UFC, saying if the money was right, "he wanted to do it."

Four days after the announcement of the settlement, Lesnar attended the K–1 HEROES mixed-martial-arts event in Las Vegas. After the final match, Lesnar got into the ring to announce that he was going to join the promotion.

Mixed martial arts message boards were abuzz with talk of Lesnar's move to mixed martial arts. The talk heated up in July when Pat Miletich told *Wrestling Observer Live* that Lesnar had been training with his team for about a week.

Miletich, who operates Miletich Fighting Systems gym in Bettendorf, Iowa, is considered by many the best MMA trainer in the country. Miletich had helped with the training of UFC welterweight champion Matt Hughes and UFC heavyweight champion Tim Silvia.

Miletich told *Wrestling Observer Live* that within a year, nobody in MMA would be able to defeat Lesnar.

It was pointed out on message boards that at age 29, Lesnar was getting a somewhat late start to his MMA career.

But *Figure Four Weekly* newsletter pointed out that, "Lesnar was an awesome natural athlete" and that "Chuck Liddell had his first fight for UFC at 28 and didn't reach his peak until his mid-30s."

The newsletter also said, "The word is that Brock learned something from his NFL and Inoki (Japan) issues and doesn't want to rush breaking into MMA (not to mention if he rushes in he's going to get beaten regularly). His attorney has been in talks with Dana White. Brock hated the long flights to Japan and would be much more open to occasionally flying to Vegas for big events. He's also learned something from WWE as he's looking for ways to market his persona in MMA."

In late July, Lesnar began his training for MMA under the guidance of Greg Nelson, who ran an MMA academy in Minnesota, and Marty Morgan, an assistant University of Minnesota wrestling coach. Nelson was hired to teach Lesnar striking and jiujitsu skills, and Morgan would oversee Lesnar's training.

Nelson, who was a gymnast in high school and a wrestler in college, is one of the top Mixed Martial Arts experts in the country. Nelson began his martial arts training as a teenager in 1983, is a certified instructor in at least three disciplines, and is a second-degree degree black belt in Brazilian jiujitsu.

Nelson opened the Minnesota Mixed Martial Arts Academy in 1992. Among the programs offered by the academy, which has at least 20 instructors, are Total Defense, Brazilian jiujitsu, Thai Kickboxing, and Mixed Martial Arts. Aside from training and teaching MMA fighters, Nelson has trained members of law enforcement agencies and military units. The MMA and Muay Thai fighters he has trained and coached have won championship titles in at least seven disciplines.

In 2002, the year Nelson was awarded a black belt, he was diagnosed with cancer—Stage IV non-Hodgkin's lymphoma. After six months of chemotherapy, the cancer was in remission. Soon after the completion of the chemotherapy, Nelson began having pain again. He returned to the Mayo Clinic in Rochester, Minnesota, where he had to be sedated because of the severe pain.

Test results showed no indication that the lymphoma had returned but didn't reveal the cause of the pain. Eventually an MRI scan revealed a slight abnormality in Nelson's upper sciatic nerve. A biopsy of the sciatic finally revealed an answer—cancer.

This time the cancer was a rare form called neurolymphomatosis. In a story about Nelson on the Mayo Clinic's website, his doctor said he had seen "only one other person with this disease in my entire career [25 years at the Mayo Clinic]." Only 33 examples of the disease were contained in medical literature.

On Memorial Day 2003—exactly one year from his first cancer diagnosis—Nelson underwent a stem-cell transplant. The transplant was a success. Subsequent tests determined that he is cancer free. Nelson resumed coaching and training fighters.

Lesnar signed a contract with the K–1 promotion on August 12, 2006. The deal was announced at the promotion's Battle of the Bellagio show in Las Vegas. The promotion said that Lesnar would make his debut sometime before the end of the year.

Meanwhile, the WWE continued to lose wrestlers. In late August, the company announced the departure of another star on its website— Kurt Angle. The announcement said, "Due to personal issues, Kurt Angle has been granted an early release his contract. WWE looks forward to establishing a new relationship with Kurt in the near future." Less than a month later, it was announced that Angle had signed with TNA.

In mid-November, K–1 announced that Lesnar would make his K–1 debut in Las Vegas in February 2007. But the debut would be delayed again. In late March, K–1 announced that Lesnar would make his debut in June.

Nelson told *Sports Illustrated* in March 2009 that Lesnar was well-suited for MMA. "He has tons of upper-body strength but also has strong hips, which help him with takedowns and positioning and footwork that [enable] him to sprawl and scramble."

Lesnar was to headline a show in Los Angeles in a five-round bout against Hong-Man Choi. K–1's attendance goal for the show—to be held June 2 in the Los Angeles Coliseum—was 100,000. Earlier that month, on March 3, UFC 68 had drawn 19,049—a record for an MMA event in North America. The main event on that card was Randy Couture's victory over Tim Silvia for the UFC heavyweight title.

K–1 teamed up with cable network Showtime to promote the Los Angeles card. Leading up to the card, Showtime aired four 30-minute shows called *Countdown to Dynamite*. Lesnar was one of the subjects featured on the first of the four broadcasts. On the broadcast, Lesnar talked about his training with Greg Nelson at the Minnesota Mixed Martial Arts Academy and said he was 30 pounds lighter than his WWE days.

A week before the event, K–1 announced that Lesnar would not be fighting Hong-Man Choi. Choi had reportedly failed a pre-fight physical for the California State Athletic Commission. It was reported that a tumor was found on a pituitary gland. Choi, who was 7'2" and weighed 319 pounds, claimed he'd had the tumor since high school and his Korean doctors had cleared him to fight. Despite Choi's assurances, the California State Athletic Commission would not allow him to fight.

Min-Soo Kim was named to replace Choi on the card. Kim, 32, who had won a silver medal in judo at the 1996 Olympics, had a 2–5 MMA record.

On June 2, 2007, with an estimated crowd of 52,000 in attendance, Lesnar's MMA debut finally arrived. In the final half-hour of the pay-per-view event, Lesnar and Kim entered the ring. Lesnar opened the match by immediately taking down Kim. Lesnar needed only 69 seconds of the scheduled five-round match (rounds were 5 minutes each) to get Kim to tap out.

After the fight, for which he was reportedly paid $500,000, Lesnar was interviewed in the ring. He said he wished he had been able to face Choi and that maybe they could eventually have a match. As for his MMA future, Lesnar said he was going to listen to offers and that he would sign with the promoter who treated him best. Kim, by the way, was paid $30,000 for his loss to Lesnar.

Figure Four Weekly provided this description of the fight: "Brock shot in and took him down immediately, which is not necessarily where you want to be with an Olympic silver medalist in judo. But Brock passed his guard easily and laid in some hard shots to the side of the head. It reminded [us], and some people won't want to hear this of Fedor [Russian mixed martial arts fighter Fedor Emelianenko], a guy who can do ungodly damage from the mount or even the guard because he's so big and so strong [and Lesnar is *much* bigger than Fedor, and probably much stronger]. Kim tapped out to the beating. For those wondering what this was like, picture Lesnar in an average WWE match where he would rush in with that scary aggression and just maul guys. That's exactly what happened here, just for real."

Prior to the event, the fighters were screened for steroids by the California State Athletic Commission. Lesnar and Kim both tested negative.

Three weeks after the event, the sports entertainment world was stunned again when it was discovered that former WWE star Chris Benoit had killed his wife and son and then himself in Fayetteville, Georgia, on June 24, 2007. Benoit, who was 40 and was booked to wrestle on a WWE pay-per-view event the weekend of his death, had been good friends with Eddie Guerrero, who had died two years earlier.

Sports Illustrated wrote that Dave Meltzer, the editor of *Wrestling Observer* newsletter who had covered professional wrestling for more than 30 years, has "carefully tabulated the death toll in his sport, and he comes up with a total of 65 wrestlers who have, since 1997, died before their 50th birthday."

On June 29, Lesnar returned to Japan to fight Kurt Angle. In front of an estimated crowd of 9,000 at Tokyo Sumo Hall, Angle defeated Lesnar via submission.

In August, *Figure Four Weekly* reported that Lesnar had met with TNA president Dixie Carter about joining the promotion. It was speculated by many that negotiations between Lesnar, the UFC, and Dana White were likely going on at this time, as well.

In late August, Lesnar did an interview with *MMA Weekly* where he said he was ready to go to work for the UFC. Lesnar told *MMA Weekly*, "We're playing the games, but I'm tired of playing the games. It's time for somebody to make a move. I'm going to go down to UFC and see what the hell is going on down there."

Lesnar said that he and White had spoken, adding, "I cannot deny or confirm anything. I'm just telling you this, I'm going to be there Saturday night [UFC 74 in Las Vegas on August 25, 2007], and I'm looking for a win. I don't care who it is. If I had to fight somebody, I'd like to fight Randy [Couture]. I'll fight Gonzaga. We'll see what happens. I hope Randy wins the fight [Couture defeated Gabriel Gonzaga to retain his UFC heavyweight title] and then I can fight him in December."

The UFC held an appeal for Lesnar.

"They're the big dog on the street," Lesnar told *MMA Weekly*. Lesnar went on to say he thought he could be a big draw for UFC. "Absolutely, no doubt in my mind."

Less than two months later, the announcement finally came. During UFC 77 on October 20, 2007, in Cincinnati, it was announced that Lesnar had signed a two-year contract with the promotion. At a press conference announcing the agreement, White said Lesnar would make his debut in February against an opponent to be determined.

Some MMA observers immediately speculated that Lesnar's first UFC opponent would be Brad Imes, but in mid-November, it was announced that Lesnar's first opponent would be former UFC heavyweight champion Frank Mir.

CHAPTER 8

THE UFC

Lesnar joined UFC at a time when the promotion was growing very successful. By 2008, UFC's worth, according to *Forbes* magazine, was $1 billion. But the organization nearly didn't survive its humble beginnings.

The UFC started in 1993 with a single-event tournament in Denver, Colorado. The promoters wanted to find the best fighters regardless of style—boxing, kick-boxing, karate, wrestling, or other martial arts styles—and advertised the event as a "no holds barred" event.

From the outset, UFC quickly received criticism for its violent contests. It was called "human cock-fighting" by a U.S. Senator and "legalized street fighting" by other critics. Many states refused to sanction the organization's events.

In 1996, Senator John McCain of Arizona, who was a fan of boxing, saw a UFC tape. He called what he saw "barbaric" and sent a letter to the governors of all 50 states, asking them to ban UFC events. By 1997, UFC events were banned in 36 states, and the UFC had been dropped by a major cable pay-per-view distributor and several individual cable television companies.

In late 2000, UFC's parent company, SEG, was nearing bankruptcy. UFC 29 was held in Tokyo, Japan, in front of an estimated 1,000 fans.

It was the last UFC event promoted by SEG. In January 2001, casino executives Frank and Lorenzo Fertitta and boxing promoter Dana White purchased the operation for $2 million. The company was given the name "Zuffa, LLC." Zuffa is an Italian word that loosely translated means "brawl," "scuffle," or "fight with no rules."

White was made the organization's chief operating officer and immediately began working to change the perception of the sport. He added more rules and more weight classes, and the sport received better marketing. The UFC had to change to survive, and it cooperated with several state athletic commissions to change its rules. In 2001, the New Jersey Athletic Control Board adopted a set of rules for UFC. The rules were accepted by other state commissions.

Although the perception of the sport was slowly improving, UFC continued to struggle financially. In the first three years under the new owners, UFC had $34 million in losses. Lesnar said on several occasions that if UFC had been more financially stable in 2000, he would have chosen UFC over professional wrestling.

A breakthrough came in January 2005, when cable network Spike TV launched *TUF*, a reality show featuring MMA fighters in competition for a UFC contract. The show was put in the time slot following WWE RAW and was a ratings success. The show's season finale, featuring a fight between competition finalists Forrest Griffin and Stephen Bonnar, is credited by White for saving the UFC.

During the next couple of years, UFC and Spike TV expanded their partnership, with the cable network picking up a weekly show called *UFC Unleashed* and broadcasting live fight events.

"Five years ago, when Spike wasn't even a year old, we were looking for a combat sport," Spike senior vice president for sports and specials Brian Diamond told the *Hollywood Reporter* in the summer of 2009. "Mixed martial arts with UFC seemed to be the best fit for us. The question was: How do we translate this to the TV screen? There were hardcore fans of the sport, but it had to grow up beyond that. The show gave you insight into who these guys were, their personalities, and characters, but more importantly, it gave you insight into them as skilled [and] highly trained athletes. This isn't easy to do. It's very real, and you have to be a certain kind of person to do that, both physically and mentally."

UFC continued to expand with the purchase of a California-based promotion called World Extreme Cagefighting in December 2006 and with the purchase of its rival—Japan-based Pride Fighting Championships—in March 2007. In 2006, UFC broke the pay-per-view industry's single-year revenue record with $222.8 million.

The mainstream media finally began to take notice as well with UFC featured on the covers of *Sports Illustrated* and *ESPN The Magazine*.

In a national teleconference with the media held June 1, White said that after taking over in 2001, "We started implementing all the things we thought could make the sport great. We started putting these incredible athletes out in front and telling their stories. You know Vince McMahon and the WWE, he creates a guy and he builds a persona for him and gives him a name. They go out and act in a certain way. These guys [in the UFC] have their own different personas, and they are interesting and real."

White told the *Hollywood Reporter* that the growth of the UFC could be attributed to "basic human interest. I can take two guys and put them in an Octagon and they can use any martial art they want and it transcends all cultural [and] language barriers. Here's the bottom line: At the end of the day, we're all human beings, and fighting is in our DNA. We get it, and we like it."

In January 2008, just three months after signing with UFC, Lesnar found himself with top billing in his first UFC event. Lesnar was set to fight Frank Mir in the main event at UFC 81 at the Mandalay Bay Events Center in Las Vegas.

Lesnar knew it meant he would again have to prove himself.

In an interview, which was posted on youtube.com less than a week before the fight, Lesnar talked about his pro wrestling days.

"There [are] still human beings in the ring, flying around, risking their lives," Lesnar said. "I mean, if you can't see that, you're very ignorant. I wrestled many matches injured, got injured, you know. There's a high risk in pro wrestling. I mean the ring is not just, you know, mom's California king-sized bed with some baler twine going around it.

"I mean, you land, you know? It's a physical ring, those guys are going out, and I was one of them, going out and slamming people and coming off the top rope and doing all these things, and I got injured for it. So there, even though, even though the outcomes may be predetermined, or even though it is 'entertainment,' these guys that are going out and putting on a show on the show that night are, they're getting hurt. I mean, not every night. But it happens. That ring is not forgiving.

"I've had many people, I own my own ring, and I've had many people in the ring and [they say] 'Oh, give me a body slam.' Okay. Then I body slam them and they're like, 'Oh, you know, I'm never doing that again. That thing is hard. What did you do to this thing?' I'm like, 'That's what I worked on, five nights a week.' That same feeling, you know?"

"That ring is not forgiving."
—Brock Lesnar

Lesnar finished the interview by talking about his rivalry with Kurt Angle.

"When me and Kurt Angle got in the square circle together, there were a lot of real things going on in there," Lesnar said. "We pushed each other to the limit every time. [He's] one of those guys that I felt like me and him could go out and not only tear the house down, but execute things and make them, and they were very real, some nights, they were very real. Kurt had neck problems way back, but I threw Kurt into the turnbuckle and came in and hit him very hard, and I believe, actually, that was where his first re-fracture in the wrestling business came from—me. I broke his neck that night. And, I wasn't the first one to break his neck, I mean he initially did, but, so it was kind of hard, me and Kurt went at it, you know? He hit me hard and I hit him back harder."

In an interview with ESPN.com several days before the fight, Lesnar said, "There are some people who disapprove of where I'm at on the card because of who I am. There is going to be a lot of animosity toward me because of the visibility that I have."

The day before the fight, the *Los Angeles Times* previewed the match by saying there was "a lot of skepticism about Lesnar and the fight." The newspaper asked, "Was it just a novelty to bring in a former WWE champion and pit him against [former UFC heavyweight champion] Mir?" The paper also asked, "If Lesnar wins, what does that say about UFC competition?"

Tim Silvia, who Mir defeated for the UFC heavyweight title in 2004, told the newspaper that Lesnar was originally "babied" in practices (in 2007) with other UFC fighters. Silvia said he believed "there are several peers and intent MMA watchers who know he is going to get beat."

But the preview pointed out that "Credentials in real wrestling are considered the essential foundation of an MMA fighter's skill set."

The newspaper also reminded readers that Lesnar had a marketable name, which the UFC needed because it had lost "popular heavyweight Randy Couture to a contract dispute [the UFC was suing Couture]."

A preview in the *Orange County Register* on the day of the fight said, "Internet message boards have been full of people imploring Mir to strike a blow for real fighters. However, that is unfair to Lesnar, who has impeccable amateur wrestling credentials, that is how the fight is being viewed by much of the public. It doesn't matter that many mixed martial artists from the U.S. come into the sport with an amateur background."

Craig Borsari, the senior vice president of operations and production for UFC, told ESPN.com, "What made us throw Brock into a fight with a guy like Frank Mir, who is a very accomplished fighter in this sport, is his amateur wrestling. Yeah, he's very well known for his professional wrestling, but he is a guy who is extremely athletic and has accomplished a lot in NCAA wrestling. He was a Division I champ, and it goes a long way to giving him credibility as a fighter."

Mir wasn't one of those taking Lesnar's UFC debut lightly.

"He has legitimate roots to be a MMA fighter," Mir told ESPN.com. "Even if he'd never had a career in pro wrestling, he would have been an MMA fighter. He has all the tools and credentials to be on that platform."

Lesnar, who had been training in MMA for nearly two years, told ESPN.com, "[The stand-up] is something I've physically worked on and mentally worked on from the very beginning. In this sport I know I have to be well-rounded, so my wrestling has had to take a backseat because I wanted to become very comfortable with my striking game and on the ground, as well. That's what we've been focusing on, my hands and the ground game.

"I'm taking this very seriously. Obviously, I'm going to have a lot to prove. There are people gunning for me, others cheering for me. That's the battle of the beast. There's always somebody [who's] got their favorite.

"I've got to come out and prove myself, even to the other fighters. I've got a lot to prove. All I have to do right now is shut up and play ball and keep on proving myself."

Going against an accomplished fighter like Mir in his first fight was the initial step in that process.

The 28-year-old Mir brought a 10–3 record into the fight. The *Los Angeles Times* said, "Submission skills have served [the 6'1", 240-pound] Mir against bigger, stronger fighters."

After defeating the 6'8", 260-pound Silvia for the title—Mir caught Silvia in an "arm bar"—Mir relinquished the title after suffering injuries in a motorcycle accident.

Mir was giving away 25 pounds to Lesnar, who had to cut weight to reach the 265-pound limit. But the *Bismarck Tribune* said that "With his jiujitsu skills, Mir is comfortable working from his back."

Mir told the newspaper, "Brock is a superior wrestler, so in a sense, where he wants to fight is where it's going to be fought at. Obviously Brock Lesnar is stronger than I am. It doesn't take a genius to figure that out. He's stronger than most anybody. If I just stand there, I'm going to get crushed."

Lesnar said, "Competition is in my blood, and I've done it for a number of years, whether it's on a wrestling mat, it's in the ring, or in an octagon. It's going to be different when the door closes on the octagon. It's me and one other man out there, and I've been in those positions before."

In his UFC debut, Lesnar immediately showed the Mandalay Bay crowd of 10,583 his strength and potential.

From the outset of the match, Lesnar dominated the action, taking down Mir. He appeared on the brink of a quick victory when the bout was briefly stopped by referee Steve Mazzagatti after Lesnar hit Mir in the back of the head. Mazzagatti stood the fighters up, and deducted a point from Lesnar for an illegal strike. After the interruption, Mir used his jiujitsu skills to catch Lesnar in a kneebar, and Lesnar was forced to submit. The match lasted 80 seconds. Lesnar had dominated the action for all but 10 seconds of the match.

At a post-match press conference, White said, "The question surrounding this event was—'Can Brock Lesnar fight?' And I think the answer is 'Yes, he can.'"

Figure Four Weekly recapped the fight, "For 80 seconds this was [Lesnar's] fight, and there are people who believe that without the referee stoppage, it would have ended after the initial flurry with Brock getting his hand raised. The place went bonkers for both the fight and the submission. It was David versus Goliath. Man versus beast, and the man was getting hammered into oblivion and managed to capitalize on a single mistake the monster made to get the victory."

In a subsequent interview with *Maxim* magazine, Lesnar was critical of Mazzagatti, saying he had made a mistake in stopping the fight.

"Frank knows deep down that he lost that fight," Lesnar said. "He got a Christmas present."

White agreed with Lesnar, saying in the same article, "That referee has no business being in this business."

The controversy surrounding the fight was whether Mazzagatti had issued Lesnar a warning before the fight was stopped.

Mazzagatti, who worked his first UFC event at UFC 43 in June 2003, explained himself in an interview with Dann Stupp of mmajunkie.com.

"Yeah, I did [issue a warning]," Mazzagatti said. "Brock's excited. It's a big, big opportunity for him, and—in my opinion—he looked down and saw the head there and he took three shots at him and caught him. I jump in and say, 'Don't hit at the back of the head.' A few more seconds go by, Mir tucks up under there again, and Brock comes down with the second couple hits to the back of the head. That's when I jumped in and had to do my job. That's what I saw."

Mazzagatti, a Las Vegas firefighter, was asked if he thought Lesnar had heard the warning.

"I don't know. I can't say that he heard it," Mazzagatti said. "I yelled it loud enough for them to hear. It was awfully loud. I yelled it, though. I've got kids, so I know how to yell. I used to be in a rock band, so I've got some lungs. But can you imagine the decibels in there? That was one of the fights everyone came to see. Of course, I came home and did my homework, watched the tape, and I can't hear myself give the warning. I couldn't hear myself say, 'Bring it on' on that beginning, [either]. That's my thing. I always shout that. If you watch the tape, you can barely even hear that."

For his debut, Lesnar was paid $250,000 according to the Nevada State Athletic Commission, but he missed out on a $200,000 victory bonus. Mir was paid $140,000, which included a $40,000 bonus for the victory and a $60,000 bonus for submission of the night.

Besides showing ability and potential as a UFC fighter, Lesnar also proved to be valuable to the promotion. The event, called Breaking Point, had an estimated 600,000 pay-per-view buys—the most for a fight card in 2008.

For his second UFC fight, Lesnar returned to Minneapolis. The fight, scheduled for August 2008, featured Heath Herring as his opponent.

In late July, Lesnar was interviewed on the UFC's website. Asked about the loss to Mir, Lesnar said, "I'm still disgusted with myself. I got so excited, then for Mazzagatti to stop the fight kinda threw a monkey wrench into my rhythm a little bit, and thus you chalk it up to a little bit of inexperience. I had Frank on the mat and then I stood up, which was pretty foolish of me. I think Frank will be the first one to admit that I had him up against the ropes, and I think he was scared."

In a conference call a week before the fight in Minneapolis, Lesnar said he considered the loss to Mir a "valuable learning experience," one that taught him he "needed to fight with control and pace himself and not get over-excited."

Lesnar said the key "was understanding that I've got 15 minutes to try and win a bout. I really rushed that fight and made a foolish mistake. I had Frank in a dominant position, and I stood up and fed him a foolish, amateur mistake."

Lesnar said he had learned to be "a more controlled fighter, and a little more relaxed in there."

At UFC 87, in his second UFC bout, Lesnar would be facing an

MMA fight veteran. Herring, 30, had spent a lot of time in Japan's Pride Fighting Championships. Herring had a 29–13–1 MMA record. Three of his losses were to Antonio Rodrigo Nogueira, the interim UFC heavyweight title holder.

The event, dubbed Seek and Destroy, was the first UFC event to be held in Minnesota since the state had sanctioned MMA events the previous year.

There were no mistakes from Lesnar in his second UFC fight, as he pummeled Herring from the outset. The fight, which was almost stopped in the first round, ended in the third round.

The Target Center crowd of 15,042, which produced a gross of $2.252 million from ticket prices that ranged from $50 to $600, voiced its approval of Lesnar.

At the post-fight press conference White said, "I'm telling you, I'm blown away by his performance tonight. I'll be honest, I didn't think he could come in and fight on this level, and he proved me wrong. One of our guys said it looks like he's hitting him with lunch boxes, his hands were so big."

Shortly after the victory over Herring, it was announced that University of Minnesota assistant wrestling coach Marty Morgan was leaving that position to become Lesnar's full-time trainer. Morgan, an assistant coach at Minnesota for 16 years, had been working informally with Lesnar.

"I've been working with Brock the past few years on his training, and now I've been offered a unique opportunity to work with him full time," Morgan said in a prepared statement released by the school.

Morgan, a Bloomington, Minnesota, native, had a tremendous body of college and international wrestling experience to draw from. Morgan, who had 11 siblings, had grown up around wrestling. Two older brothers—John and Gordy—competed on U.S. Olympic teams. John Morgan represented the United States at the Seoul Olympics in 1988, and Gordy Morgan was on the 1996 Olympic team.

Marty Morgan started his college wrestling career at North Dakota State. As a freshman, Morgan won an NCAA Division II championship. After his freshman year, he transferred to the University of Minnesota. For the Gophers, Morgan was a three-time All-America and a two-time NCAA finalist. As a sophomore in 1989, he finished sixth at 167 pounds at the NCAA Division I meet. As a junior, Morgan set a Minnesota school single-season record with 20 pins and was the NCAA runner-up at 177 pounds. As a senior, Morgan became the first wrestler in school history to go unbeaten (39–0) and capped his season by winning the NCAA Division I 177-pound championship. In his three seasons at Minnesota, Morgan won 110-of-122 matches.

Following his college career, Morgan, who earned B.A. and M.A. degrees in education from the University of Minnesota, was a two-time Greco-Roman national champion, and he participated in the World Championships. He was third at the U.S. Olympic Trials in 1992 and fourth at the 1996 U.S. Olympic Trials.

In 1993, Morgan became an assistant coach at his alma mater. Three years later, he was promoted to head assistant coach. He held that position for the next 13 years.

"This has been a difficult decision," Morgan said in the statement, "considering that I have been involved with the program for 20 years as an athlete and coach."

Gophers wrestling coach J Robinson was philosophical about Morgan's departure.

"This is a once-in-a-lifetime opportunity for him," Robinson said in the same statement. "I think it's important for people to see different opportunities that life has to offer from a different perspective."

As Lesnar's trainer, the first task facing Morgan was to get Lesnar ready for his next fight—in less than three months—against UFC heavyweight champion Randy Couture.

The fight would be the first for Couture since his return to the UFC after an 11-month legal dispute with the company. Like Lesnar,

Couture had been a successful NCAA Division I wrestler. Couture had wrestled for Oklahoma State, where he was an NCAA Division I runner-up twice. Couture also had an extensive international wrestling resume. Couture, who was 45, had a 16–9 record in MMA bouts, but he hadn't fought in nearly 15 months.

Couture was one of the UFC's legends. His first MMA fight was in 1997, and he won the UFC light heavyweight title twice and the UFC heavyweight championship three times.

The fact that Lesnar was fighting for the UFC heavyweight championship in just his third UFC fight apparently annoyed some UFC fighters, who had waited years for a similar opportunity. In an interview with the *Daily Star* newspaper in London two weeks before the fight, Lesnar was asked about the reaction.

"I'm getting sick of hearing from some dumb people [who] say I don't deserve this fight because I've only been fighting for a year," Lesnar said. "My message to them is simple: Get over it! This is a business, and people know who I am and want to see me fight."

In the same interview with the *Daily Star*, Lesnar also talked about his professional wrestling career.

"People ask me about my WWE career," Lesnar said, "but those are two years I can't remember because of painkillers and vodka. I wrestled guys weighing 500 pounds with a broken rib every night for six months, and I couldn't sleep at night without vodka. The whole thing is a blur to me."

To train for the fight against Lesnar, who outweighed him by 40 pounds, Couture said he prepared by going against several bigger sparring partners.

"I've fought with plenty of guys with Brock's size," Couture said in a prefight conference call. "Both my last two fights [against Tim Silvia and Gabriel Gonzaga] have been with guys [who] were bigger than me by at least 25 pounds."

Lesnar said that Couture, who was considered the underdog in his fight against Silvia, was a "world-class athlete. I wouldn't consider Randy an underdog."

Lesnar added, "From the day I signed with [the UFC], I said 'I want to be the heavyweight champion.' Hopefully this is a win-win for everybody. I'm coming to win this fight, and that's the bottom line."

The Lesnar-Couture fight attracted a lot of media attention. On the day of the fight, the *Los Angeles Times* reported the fight "was being billed as the biggest Ultimate Fighting Championship bout in history."

The Oklahoma City *Oklahoman* said, "There is no way to over-hype this fight. When this fight was announced in September, it was like a dream for MMA fans. This may not be the best fight ever, but [it] is certainly one of the most anticipated contests in the 15 years of the Ultimate Fighting Championship."

Dana White told a prefight teleconference, "The star power in this fight is so intense. There's buzz everywhere about Brock doing well in the UFC and can he beat Randy."

In the prefight news conference, Lesnar had told reporters that he was confident he could "reverse" Couture's knack for "getting guys on the ground and controlling them."

Couture said, "I have the skill set to deal with his size and athleticism. I don't want to lay underneath him. I don't have any concern about the layoff. An MMA layoff isn't that big of a deal because our training is so close to real competition. That's what it's all about. I'm not ready to leave yet."

WWE announcer Jim Ross was asked by the *Oklahoman* to predict the fight.

"I have huge respect for Randy Couture," Ross said, "but at 45 years of age and giving up approximately 55 pounds come fight time, I'm predicting a Brock Lesnar win. I think Randy can win if Lesnar gets careless and Couture can exploit a Lesnar mistake. The good, big man beats the legendary, smaller man."

Ross also recalled Lesnar's WWE days. "We had to restrain Lesnar from doing the more athletic, aerial maneuvers that smaller wrestlers once had the marker on. Lesnar's natural balance and coordination gave him the ability to execute maneuvers that 300-pounders rarely attempted."

On November 15, 2008, in front of a crowd of 14,272 at the MGM Grand Garden Arena, Lesnar didn't make any mistakes. Lesnar needed less than two rounds to defeat Couture, dropping him with a right behind his ear. The referee stopped the fight at 3:07 of the second round.

Couture told a postfight press conference, "I still feel like I'm getting better as a fighter. But those were big ham hocks coming at me. He's a big guy, and he caught me with a big shot."

Before Lesnar dropped Couture, Couture had landed a right in the second round that caused a cut above Lesnar's right eye.

Lesnar told the press, "I'll only get better. I'm going to keep molding myself into a dominating fighter. You have to be a well-rounded fighter in this day and age, but I'm in a dream right now. This is awesome."

> ## "You have to be a well-rounded fighter in this day and age."
> —Brock Lesnar

White said that Lesnar had "showed the MMA world" that he "is for real, and his combination of speed and power is absolutely devastating. When he came over to us, he told me he just wanted to fight the best in the world, and that is just what he has done. Now that he has that title after overcoming someone of the incredible stature of Randy Couture, so you know that he really does mean business."

For the fight, Lesnar earned $450,000 which included a bonus of $200,000 for the victory. Couture was paid $250,000.

In the 2009 paperback edition of his autobiography, *Becoming the Natural: My Life In and Out of the Cage*, Couture wrote, "And then it happened. One of those daddy-longlegs arms came at me. And I slipped it, but it just kept unfolding. It clipped me behind my ear, and I went down. Lesnar was on me in a nanosecond, and his fists rained down on me like a large woman swinging a purse. No matter which way I turned, there was nowhere to go. And then it was over."

In an interview with *UFC Magazine* in late 2009, Lesnar was asked, "When was the last time you got rocked training or fighting?"

Lesnar told the magazine, "I've been hit. Randy [Couture] hit me and gave me a good shot. Mir caught me with a knee. I wouldn't say rocked. I don't think I've been rocked yet. I took a leg kick once in training camp and was unprepared for it. I've been hit. We spar hard, but other than that, I can't really say. Getting rocked? Never."

Less than a week after the victory over Couture, Lesnar was back at the Target Center in Minneapolis—the site of his first UFC victory— as a spectator. Lesnar was one of 19,107 in attendance to watch the Minnesota Timberwolves take on the defending NBA champion Boston Celtics and former Timberwolves star Kevin Garnett. The Timberwolves led by three at halftime but were outscored by the Celtics' 35–10 in the third quarter.

The Timberwolves' third-quarter performance prompted columnist Patrick Reusse to write in the next day's *Minneapolis Star Tribune*, "Clearly, in all his hellacious battles with heavyweights from Iowa and Oklahoma State and in all the blood baths choreographed by Vince McMahon, and even in his short time inside the Octagon, Lesnar had never been exposed to the gore, to the carnage, that took place as those 12 minutes crawled off the Target Center's scoreboard clock."

L. Jon Wertheim wrote in *Sports Illustrated* the week after Lesnar's victory over Couture that Lesnar's victory was a positive thing for UFC "Barely a month after Kimbo Slice proved himself unworthy of his considerable hype, another mixed martial arts curiosity, Brock Lesnar, validated himself. Last Saturday in Las Vegas, Lesnar poleaxed the venerable Randy Couture to become the UFC's heavyweight champ. The skeptics who'd looked down on Lesnar's WWE pedigree and his quick ascent—he was given a title shot in his third UFC fight—are no longer questioning his bona fides. Lesnar showed an ability to throw and withstand punches and, befitting a former NCAA wrestling champ [at Minnesota], defend the takedown. 'Guys aren't just big anymore; they're good athletes,' Couture, 45, conceded after the fight. 'Brock is a great indication of where the division is going.'

"This is good news for the UFC. Despite its explosive growth, there have been concerns about its supply of marketable stars [read: pay-per-view engines]. Couture, Chuck Liddell, and Tito Ortiz, the three biggest names in the sport, are nearing the final rounds of their careers. In Lesnar, a 31-year old South Dakotan, the UFC has a new face—bloodstained though it may be."

In an interview with *Inside MMA* two weeks after the fight, Couture said he hoped a rematch with Lesnar was in the future. "A rematch would be fun. I feel like I have what it takes to win that fight. You hate to see those slip away, but sometimes that happens. A rematch would be cool."

In an interview on sportsagentblog.com, MMA training expert Pat Miletich was asked if the emergence of Lesnar, with his WWE background, "compromised MMA's legitimacy at all?"

"Not at all," Miletich said. "People need to understand, and I think they do, that most WWE athletes are great athletes. Brock Lesnar was a Division I national champion wrestler. That doesn't happen by accident. He's a tremendous athlete."

The next order of business for Lesnar was to prepare for the winner of the upcoming fight between Frank Mir and Antonio Rodrigo Nogueira.

In late December 2008 at UFC 92, Mir defeated Nogueira to earn the interim heavyweight title, which had been created because of former UFC heavyweight champion Randy Couture's departure from the company. A fight with Lesnar to unify the title would take place sometime in the upcoming year.

The fight with Mir was originally scheduled for UFC 98 on May 23, 2009, in Las Vegas. But Mir suffered a knee injury during training that required surgery to remove bone chips. The fight was rescheduled for July 11—the day before Lesnar's birthday—in Las Vegas. The pay-per-view event from the Mandalay Bay resort would be the 100th in UFC's 16-year history. Lesnar was obviously motivated for his rematch with Mir, who had an 18–2 record after becoming the UFC fighter to defeat Nogueira with a second-round TKO.

In an interview with HDNet on June 24, Lesnar said, "You know life is about timing, and this is the right time for me to be a mixed martial artist, and I really feel like this is my career I'm supposed to be doing. Had it been around, had it been the opportunity…I wouldn't change a thing. I've had to evolve and re-create myself, pretty much. Here I was labeled as a professional wrestler and entertainer. Nobody really took me seriously.

"The hardest part for me was to find the right guys to train me and understand me. Because I think I understand myself as an athlete, you know, that I'm capable of…I'm very coachable. And to find the right people to coach me was probably the hardest thing."

"The only thing that I've got going for me is Frank's got a win over me, and I don't like to lose," Lesnar told the *St. Paul Pioneer Press* a few days before the fight. "Revenge is a key factor for me here."

Despite having defeated Lesnar in their first meeting, Mir was considered by Las Vegas Sports Books to be the underdog in the rematch.

"After the Nogueira fight, I thought I wouldn't be the underdog," Mir, a Las Vegas resident, told the *Orange County (Calif.) Register*. "My friends and I were speaking afterwards and, obviously being a

Vegas person, we were talking about the sports books and the odds. I was like, 'Nah, guys. I'm not going to be the underdog.' When the odds came out [Lesnar was a 2.5:1 favorite], I was like, 'What can I say? Go bet guys, it's your money.'"

While Mir was surprised by the odds, he understood the public's fascination with Lesnar.

"I think people still judge a lot on potential, and people are visual creatures and they see Lesnar," Mir told the *Register*. "Obviously, if the two of us are standing at a bar, I'd probably pick on me before I pick on him."

The victory over Nogueira capped a tremendous professional comeback for Mir, who didn't fight for nearly 17 months after suffering a broken femur and torn knee ligaments in a motorcycle accident in September 2004. After returning to the Octagon in February 2006, Mir fought several times before missing much of 2007 because of a shoulder injury.

Mir told the *Orange County Register* that he was 14 and a freshman in high school when he and his father watched the telecast of UFC 1. Mir said, "That first UFC show was an eye-opening experience for me."

In the May issue of *Maxim* magazine, Mir said, "If Brock Lesnar was never in the WWE, he would have never have gotten a title shot. And he knows that. But that's how people get paid. The bottom line is it's not always about who's a better fighter. All I remember from last time is him whimpering and wincing as I was tapping him. Through the grapevine we found out that Brock hired lawyers to look over officiating rules, but they couldn't find nothing wrong with any of it. I look at it as a great victory. He couldn't put me away with his power. Brock was trying to win the fight real quickly by landing a couple of shots and not doing damage. That's not really an honorable way to try to win."

Mir went on to say that he had studied Lesnar's career all the way back to college. "If you watched when he wrestled in college, his abilities were not very technical. He used his size and power. He won matches by one and two points, drew the pace down, got real boring."

Mir told the magazine that Lesnar fundamentally remained the same kind of fighter and that Lesnar's strategy would play into his submission skills. "There's no way anybody can roll with me for 25 minutes and not get tapped. It's just impossible."

The magazine said that White called Mir "one of the two greatest heavyweight submission guys ever."

In a prefight teleconference, Mir toned down the rhetoric and told reporters that he was "prepared for the worst Brock Lesnar anybody could imagine. I have to [be]."

Mir acknowledged that Lesnar had improved as an MMA fighter in the 17 months since their first meeting, saying that in addition to his wrestling skills, Lesnar had developed his "striking" skills.

"We just went ahead and prepared for the worst-case scenario that Brock knows everything I know about mixed martial arts," Mir said. "And, on top of that, he's stronger and bigger and faster than I am.'

Lesnar told the teleconference that his improvement showed "the ability to evolve. I could have been very pigheaded when I made this transition from a pro wrestler to an ultimate fighter and said, 'Well, I'm just going to use my wrestling technique and my strength and speed.' That would have been very ignorant of me to do so. The ability for me to have an open mind and an open game plan, you know to keep my eyes and ears open and my mouth shut and acquire the right people around me to train me."

In an interview with AskMen.com before the fight, Lesnar was asked what fighting styles he focused on when training for the rematch with Mir.

"Actually, I don't focus on a lot of wrestling," Lesnar said. "I have 18 years of wrestling training, I mean we touch on it a little bit, but I want to solidify my stand-up fighting and my ground game. I'm not a wrestler anymore. I'm a fighter, and that's what I'm going to show in this fight. My strength is my wrestling, but I don't focus on it as much. I try to focus on a lot of different things like knees, elbows, submissions, and submission defense—just a lot of different things."

Asked in the interview what schedule he was following, Lesnar responded, "We have a couple of workouts today—we're really bringing things together now, the calm before the storm, making sure my body has plenty of rest and that my body is down to the weight it needs to be. I'm always staying motivated because as training camp goes on, practices become more intense, harder and shorter. It's a mental thing, too, not only physical—you have to stay mentally sharp and stay focused on the task in front of you."

Lesnar went on to say that in a normal day, he trained "about four to six hours. Every day is different. I listen to my body. Some days I'll work out once, and others I'll do more. It depends on what we need to get accomplished during the week and if we get enough done and we feel good about ourselves. There's a science about it."

Lesnar was asked if he had any tips for the website's readers and their own training.

"Stay open-minded," Lesnar said. "Stay focused. Train hard and train smart. For me, the older I get, the smarter I have to train also because the recovery time is longer. Work on everything, become a well-rounded fighter—don't just be good at one thing, be good at everything."

Asked if it was difficult to cut weight to reach the 265-pound limit for UFC heavyweights, Lesnar said, "No, not really. I'm not worried about it. Right now I'm trying to shed the pounds off and get back at 265. I started camp at 285, so I'm slowly shedding off the weight with lots of protein, good carbs, and lots of water."

Mir admitted that it had been difficult to prepare for the rematch with Lesnar. During his training for the fight, he went against training partners who were 6'7" or 6'8" to prepare for Lesnar's 83-inch reach.

"I remember even watching [Couture], when he slipped that punch from Brock, he thought he was out of the way," Mir said. "And that punch kept on coming and it kept on coming and it kept on coming, and finally it just—it hit him and it caught him and he went down."

Aside from Lesnar's reach, Mir said Lesnar's size and speed were also difficult to handle.

"That's the one thing that I really took from my first fight that I made sure I trained for, for this fight, was there was times when I was on the ground that I lost him," Mir said. "I was like, 'He's on my right side. He's punching me…where'd he go? He's on my left side.' And I had to watch the tape to actually see what happened and watch him rotate from one side of my hips to the other."

Watching tapes of Lesnar's subsequent three fights showed Mir how much Lesnar had matured as a fighter.

"They're hard to watch tape on because you don't know how much more he's going to improve every fight," Mir said. "From Heath to Randy, you see him very composed, standing in front. I remember my trainers were sort of like, 'Hey man, is he just standing there and actually fighting strike for strike instead of just bull rushing across the cage?' That only took one fight to fix that. So it makes it a little more difficult on my part to actually sit there and assess what we're going to prepare for."

Lesnar said he had trained hard for his first title defense.

"We've spent a lot of time in the gym, a lot of time watching film, a lot of blood, a lot of sweat, a lot of tears," Lesnar said. "This training camp was a very hard, very hard training camp. That's the hardest part, I'm just looking forward to the fight.… To me, getting in there and actually doing exactly what you love to do is an honor and a privilege."

The first round of his title defense showed what a dominating MMA fighter Lesnar had become. The opening round saw Lesnar land a flurry of punches to Mir's face that left Mir bloodied. The second round was much of the same before the referee stopped the fight at 1:48 of the round. The TKO victory improved Lesnar's MMA won-lost record to 4–1.

But the stoppage of the fight wasn't the end of the action in the ring. Immediately after the end of the fight, Lesnar went up to Mir and began taunting him. The Mandalay Bay crowd of 10,871 booed Lesnar, who responded by making obscene gestures toward the fans with both hands.

In the postfight interview in the ring, Lesnar made a crude remark and insulted one of UFC's top sponsors by saying he would enjoy a beverage from one of the sponsor's rivals. He continued with more insults of Mir. As the fans continued to boo Lesnar, he responded by saying, "I love it."

White blasted Lesnar for his actions in the post-fight press conference. "That's not who Brock really is, and what he did out there is not real," White told the media. "You don't have to act like someone you're not. This isn't the WWE. I'm not trying to get someone to act all crazy so we'll do more pay-per-views. That's not what this sport is about."

Lesnar said, "Dana came back and we had a whip-the-dog session. I screwed up, and I apologize. I was in the entertainment business for awhile, and I guess there's still a little of that in me. You guys ask me all the time if there's anything I can drag over from WWE, and I guess you've seen a little bit of that. I'm used to selling pay-per-view tickets. I come from a business that is purely entertainment. I'm just trying to do my job."

Jim Ross of the WWE, who watched the bout on pay-per-view, gave his thoughts about the event on his blog the day after the fight. "The Brock Lesnar–Frank Mir fight ended as I predicted, and that was if Lesnar did not make any careless mistakes early because he was too emotionally charged that Brock would dominate Mir. That's exactly what happened. Lesnar's size, strength, take-down ability, and punching power are challenging attributes to defend. The ability to take an opponent down, seemingly at will, ala GSP [UFC welterweight Georges St. Pierre], will always be a card Lesnar can play against anyone I've seen on the MMA horizon."

Ross also had a few things to say about Lesnar's post fight actions. "Lesnar's post-match, unscripted remarks did not completely surprise me," Ross wrote in his blog. "Those that do not personally know Lesnar as I do need to understand that his level of intensity and fury is scary. Brock has said many things in private conversations that I have been a part of that would make one do a double take. He is an intimidating, emotional jock who has been known for speaking first and thinking later.

"I don't think Brock is an inherently evil person whatsoever, but his level of competitiveness can be dangerous. It's like Brock 'moonsaulting' at Wrestlemania 19 in Seattle against Kurt Angle when being advised not to prior to the bout. Lesnar was told that men his size don't do top-rope moonsaults, which was the wrong thing to say to the former NCAA All-American and national champion. Lesnar came close to tragically ending his athletic career that night while defying logic and doing what others told him that he could not do. Lesnar, as I pointed out a couple of days ago, loves to be jeered...the louder the better. When Lesnar, who detested the travel and emotional demands of WWE's schedule, was the most 'hated villain' on the roster, he was at his happiest in sports entertainment. Plus, let's not forget that some people genuinely enjoy being a...bully. Lesnar, in a ring, mat, or octagon, embraces that persona. Brock may say that he did not like school, but the South Dakota farm boy is far from being a dumb jock. Lesnar has plenty of common sense and knows, as [WWE Raw general manager] Eric Bischoff wrote, that controversy does indeed create cash."

Ross went on to compare UFC to WWE. "UFC told a compelling story that had a 17-month arc beginning with Lesnar's first match, the tap-out loss to Mir, culminating strategically with the main event at UFC 100 that was built on the time-tested story of retribution and revenge, two basic human instincts. Long storytelling arcs are gold whether it be in MMA, boxing, or pro wrestling. Lesnar is seemingly so detested right now by MMA purists and fanatics that they will continue to pay big money to see someone humble Lesnar. Even the Russian, Fedor, will likely be the crowd favorite against Lesnar if that fight ever happens. Bottom line is the next man to beat Lesnar is made."

Ross concluded his post by writing, "My feedback to UFC 100 is normally not taken well within the MMA community, because I'm a 'Pro Wrestling Guy' you know, but I am a sports fan and am simply offering one paying customer's point of view."

The day after the fight—his 32nd birthday—Lesnar told the *Minneapolis Star Tribune* that he was sorry.

"What I meant by 'I love it,' I just love being in the Octagon," Lesnar said. "Cheer for me, boo me. I just love being in the moment right now. You know I do want to apologize to the young kids watching. My emotions got the best of me, especially for the hand gestures. I have fun doing this. I think that people who walked away from the television set…were fully entertained and they didn't feel like they paid too much to watch UFC 100."

But Lesnar didn't apologize for all of his actions.

"I guess after waiting 17 months, having a guy beat you and on top of that being a sore loser…this was a big revenge fight for me," Lesnar told the *Minneapolis Star Tribune*. "There was a lot of built-in emotion from deep inside, most definitely. Things got a little crazy there at the end."

Lesnar was paid $400,000 for the fight, while Mir was paid $45,000. The event had a UFC-record 1.6 million pay-per-view buys.

After the fight, speculation immediately began about who would be Lesnar's next opponent. White told the post-fight press conference that "Eventually, Fedor is going to be here."

White was referring to Fedor Emelianenko, a Russian heavyweight who was fighting for the Affliction promotion. Emelianenko, considered by many the top MMA heavyweight in the world, had a 30–1 record. UFC and White had tried to reach a contract with Emelianenko on several occasions with no success.

White said, "We'll end up getting that deal done, and then we'll do Brock vs. Fedor and it will be a huge fight."

Having chewed out Lesnar for his post fight antics, White then praised Lesnar. "This guy is a phenomenal athlete, and he gets better every time. He might be the greatest heavyweight champion in history."

It soon became apparent that a Lesnar-Emelianenko fight wouldn't happen any time soon. The next scheduled fight for Emelianenko, who had fought most of his fights for Japanese promoter Pride before it was purchased by UFC, was against Josh Barnett in an Affliction promotion. That bout was canceled after Barnett failed a drug test and was suspended. Affliction soon announced that it would no longer promote any fight cards.

UFC renewed its efforts to sign Emelianenko. But negotiations failed when UFC wouldn't agree to be a co-promoter with M–1 Global, which Emelianenko had a financial interest in. In August, the Russian heavyweight signed to fight undefeated Minnesotan Brett Rogers for Strikeforce on November 7.

Two weeks after signing with the California-based promotion, Emelianenko was quoted in an article about the UFC in *Slate*, an online magazine. "The UFC's attitude toward fighters is not a good one. They don't treat them like human beings."

The *Slate* article concluded, "UFC's failure to sign Emelianenko is a sign of what lies ahead as MMA continues to grow as a sport and as fighters become more famous. For right now, the sport's champions might be happy to fight on commission, but they won't always be—fighters who draw, like Mike Tyson, are going to want to be paid like Mike Tyson, and rightly so. The heavyweight champion [Emelianenko] probably won't be the last fighter to complain about UFC's policy, and he won't be the last one who's able to do something about it. As for the champ himself? His Strikeforce deal will be up in about a year, and then we'll get to do this all over again."

Lesnar was scheduled to defend his title against unbeaten Shane Carwin on November 21, 2009, as part of UFC 106 in Las Vegas.

Carwin, who holds two college degrees—in environmental technology and in mechanical engineering—and works for the North Weld

County Water District in Colorado, was also critical of Lesnar's post-fight display at UFC 100.

Carwin, who was an All-America in football and wrestling at Western Colorado State and is a volunteer wrestling coach at the University of Northern Colorado, wrote in his blog, "The flipping off of the fans that just lined your pocket with millions of dollars is just lame. He may be a champion, but he has a long ways to go before he earns the respect of a champion.... We have no scripts in this sport, no predetermined earning amount and no predetermined outcomes. It doesn't matter if you win or lose; it matters how you win or lose."

In a subsequent interview posted on Sportsnet.ca in the first week of September, Carwin said, "Lesnar is a talented athlete and very gifted. And I said he would excel in the UFC. I know some of his antics have been questioned and questioned by me. I know I came out and said a few things about that, that's it's not who we are as MMA fighters. I felt that it was appropriate for some of the MMA fighters to speak out and just say who we are and what we're about. That's definitely not the perception I want people to see me as."

Carwin added he was looking forward to the fight with Lesnar. "I'm very fortunate. I'm excited for the opportunity. It's a great opportunity. And I'm going to make the most of it. But, you know, not to take anything away from Brock, he's a great wrestler. I know he's a great wrestler. So I'll train for that. You know, the other areas that come into play.... I have a great striking coach and that's my passion now, is the boxing. I like being on the feet. I like to, you know, throw bombs and get in those exchanges and work on my feet. So, you know, maybe I have a bit of an advantage there. Um, on the ground, we'll see. It's going to be an interesting fight. I know it's going to be an exciting fight. I don't expect it to go five rounds."

One problem the 6'3" Lesnar presented to UFC fighters was his 83-inch reach. Carwin, who has an 80-inch reach, downplayed Lesnar's advantage.

"You know, I don't think it matters," Carwin said. "We'll take it anywhere it goes. And work from there. That's something that, I think, all mixed martial artists work for is to be comfortable in all areas of their game. And it's something that we strive for. When it comes to jiu-jitsu and being on my back, that's where I spend most of the time on in practice. We're out here right now, game-planning and working on a few things, and, obviously, that's going to be in the arsenal."

CHAPTER 9

UNCERTAINTY

But less than a month before UFC 106, White announced that the Lesnar-Carwin fight would be postponed until January 2010 because of an undisclosed illness to Lesnar.

On October 26, 2009, White told Yahoo! Sports that Lesnar had been sick for more than three weeks and, "He [Lesnar] said he's never been this sick in his life. He said it's been going on for a long time, and he just wasn't able to shake it."

Brian Stegeman, Lesnar's agent, told Yahoo! Sports, "Honestly, he's been sick since the beginning of this camp, and he's had to take days off throughout."

Stegeman added, "We kept thinking that he'd get better and be back at it, but it finally got to a point here where we were looking at a situation where Brock would have just two weeks to train for this fight. That's just not fair to him. There's no way a two-week training camp is even close to being fair to him, and we all recognized that. We kept hoping Brock would respond and get better, but it just lingered."

The UFC announced that the Lesnar-Carwin main event would be replaced by a fight between Tito Ortiz and Forrest Griffin.

Little else was announced about Lesnar's illness. Fueling the mystery was that Lesnar was on the Metrodome sidelines in Minneapolis on October 18 for the Minnesota Vikings–Baltimore Ravens game and appeared healthy.

On November 4, it was announced that the Lesnar-Carwin fight would be pushed back indefinitely because Lesnar had been diagnosed with mononucleosis. The next week, several media outlets reported that Lesnar had been hospitalized after collapsing during a hunting trip to Canada.

Following UFC 105 in Las Vegas on November 14, White was asked for an update on Lesnar's medical condition. White told reporters that Lesnar's condition had "worsened" but while Lesnar didn't have "AIDS" or "cancer," he wouldn't be able to fight any time soon.

White wouldn't confirm if or where Lesnar was hospitalized but did say he had urged the heavyweight champion to see doctors at the Mayo Clinic in Rochester, Minnesota.

On Monday, November 16, with several Internet sites reporting that Lesnar was in a "fight for his life," UFC spokesman Joe Fernandez emailed reporters to say the organization would have an update on Lesnar the next day. Fernandez said, "We will definitely know something on Brock by Tuesday."

Also on November 16, White told reporters that Lesnar was recovering from a "bacterial infection in his intestinal tract."

The situation was cleared up the next day when White announced via Twitter, "Brock had minor surgery and is feeling better. Not 100 percent sure he is out of the woods, but feeling better."

Following the procedure, which was performed in Bismarck, North Dakota, Lesnar returned to his home in Minnesota. Lesnar's MMA trainer, Greg Nelson, told the *Minneapolis Star Tribune* that Lesnar "knew something was wrong when he began dropping weight more rapidly than expected in training."

White told Yahoo! Sports that Lesnar's long-term future with the organization was still in doubt. "We don't know if he'll ever fight again."

White said that Lesnar would visit the Mayo Clinic for more tests. "He had a hole in his intestine," White told the website. "The [stuff] was leaking into his stomach. That's what was causing him so much pain. That and he had abscesses. The doctor told him he hadn't been right for a year. His immune system had been trying to fight this thing, and that's why he was susceptible to getting sick.

"We find out more next week. I don't know what to say. It's been better now than last week, but what that means, I don't know."

Envisioning Lesnar's return to fighting, White said, "If he's done what he's done at less than 100 percent, then imagine how he'll be if he is 100 percent."

In early January 2010, White told reporters that Lesnar's future in fighting would become more clear after Lesnar's recovery and progress was evaluated by doctors.

White told Loretta Hunt of Sherdog.com, a website devoted to mixed martial arts, "This week, I'll know. If the doctors say things are going well and things are going in the right direction, then maybe we're a few months away [from Lesnar's return]. If it's not...he'll have to retire, or he'll be out for a couple of years."

White said there was still the possibility that Lesnar could need more surgery.

"If he has to have this major surgery, we're talking about the quality of this guy's life forever," White said. "I like him. I respect him. I hope that doesn't happen for him and his family's sake. Pay-per-view buys...I don't give a [expletive] about that. I hope the guy's okay."

White also announced that Carwin and Mir would meet for the interim heavyweight title at UFC 111 on March 27 in Newark, New Jersey.

On January 15, Nelson appeared on MMA Live, ESPN.com's weekly MMA webcast and announced that Lesnar would fight again.

"Brock Lesnar is definitely coming back to fight again," Nelson said. "He's just kinda coming up slowly, training, getting his body ready, and being smart with his recovery. He's been going into the doctor and making sure everything is going well, and he'll make sure to go in for a couple of more tests to make sure he's 100 percent ready to train when he starts."

Nelson was asked how long it would take for Lesnar to get into shape so he could begin training.

"Being the athlete that he is," Nelson said, "and you know, just a strong, tough farm guy, he's used to dealing with adversity and stuff like that. I know that he'll be able to come back faster than people expect, but we're not going to push the river at all.

"We want him to be 100 percent healthy when he starts to train, but being a tough guy and being an athlete for the majority of his life, he's been able to deal with adversity like this and other things, so I'm sure once he gets going he'll be at the top of his game real quick."

Lesnar finally talked to the media on January 20 and said he was ready to resume training.

"I got very, very sick," Lesnar told ESPN. "It was a challenging time for me. I thought that I was...my career was ended. Luckily, thank God, my family, and the UFC, I'm coming back."

Lesnar said he had spent several months fighting an intestinal disorder called diverticulitis. Lesnar also dealt with an infection and mononucleosis.

"Everybody has got life-changing experiences, and this is one of them for me," Lesnar said in an interview with the Associated Press. "I believe things happen for a reason. It gave me a different perspective on my life and family. I considered myself a healthy human being, and for something like this to happen to me, I need to reevaluate. I have to make some changes."

On January 5 at the Mayo Clinic in Rochester, Lesnar had undergone a colonoscopy, which revealed that antibiotics had cleared up the infection and no further surgery would be necessary.

"The Mayo Clinic said, 'You've got a winning lottery ticket,'" Lesnar told the Associated Press.

Uncertainty

In an interview on ESPN's *SportsCenter*, Lesnar went into detail about his illness.

"I missed almost three weeks of my training camp [for the Carwin] fight. Kept going to the doctor, couldn't figure out what the problem was. Finally, it was a Monday [and] I said to my trainer I can't do this fight. I was devastated to just back out of the fight. I decided to get away and take a trip up to Canada and do some hunting. I could either stay at home and sit on the couch and climb the walls or go to Canada and do something I would enjoy. So I got up there and didn't feel right. Had a lot of severe stomach pain, and one night I woke up in severe shock, had a 104 temperature, and felt like I was shot in the guts."

Lesnar had gone bow hunting with his brother Chad. They were hunting near Cromer, Manitoba, about 75 miles west of Brandon, Manitoba, when he got sick. He was driven to a hospital in Brandon, Manitoba, where he was hospitalized for three days. In a report that appeared in the *Calgary Sun*, Chad Lesnar said he wanted to drive Brock to Winnipeg—about 130 miles east of Brandon—for a CT scan because the scanner at the Brandon hospital wasn't working. Chad said a doctor told him there was no need to take Brock to a Winnipeg hospital.

"I entered the hospital around 4:00 AM on a Saturday morning," Brock Lesnar said in an interview with ESPN. "And I spent two nights there. No one talks about that. Their CT machine was broken, and they were waiting for a replacement. They could not take a picture of my stomach. If they would have had the ability to take the picture, they would have seen I had holes inside me. If I had stayed at that Canadian hospital, at best I would have been retired and would have had to wear a colostomy bag. At worst, I could have died. They didn't have any state-of-the-art equipment, and I was in their facility. So first thing Monday morning, when the doctors came in and they still didn't have a way to take a picture of my stomach...still didn't have a way to operate that CT machine...my wife and I knew we had to get out of there.

"And my wife saved my life. She got me out of there and drove 100 mph to get me down to Bismarck and to Medcenter One and got me with Dr. [Brent] Bruderer and his staff, and that doctor there saved my career and my life."

Lesnar said he was in "excruciating pain" during the drive to Bismarck.

"I take my hat off to this doctor there [in Bismarck, North Dakota]," Lesnar told *Sports Center*. "They diagnosed me with diverticulitis. I had a severe case. I had a rupture of one of my diverticuli, which means I had a hole in my stomach."

Lesnar told the teleconference his lowest point during the illness was "getting care from Canada. The hospital that I was at, it wasn't their fault. They couldn't do nothing for me. It was like I was in a third-world country. I'm just stating the facts here, and that's the facts. I love Canada. I own property in Canada, but if I had to choose between getting care in Canada and the United States, I definitely want to be in the United States. Canadians, don't get me wrong here. Listen, I love Canada, some of the best people and best hunting in the world. I have family up there. But I wasn't at the right facility. And it makes sense for me to say that."

Later in the teleconference, Lesnar added, "I'm not bashing the Canadian healthcare, I'm not bashing it at all. I'm a U.S. citizen. It just so happens I was in Canada. If I would have been in Thailand or Puerto Rico, I would want to get back to the United States, in my homeland, to get my health care."

In Bismarck, he had fluid drained from three pockets that had formed in his stomach, and he was placed on antibiotics. Doctors told him that if the antibiotics didn't work, he was faced with the possibility of having part of his colon removed. Doctors said his chances of fighting again after surgery were less than 50 percent.

"I was in the hospital for 11 days, no food, no water, fed intravenously, lost 40 pounds, got out of the hospital, went home, and decided I wanted a second opinion," Lesnar said. "Went down to the Mayo Clinic in Rochester, both doctors in Bismarck and the Mayo Clinic diagnosed me and said I need surgery. I need my colon removed, but we can't until the swelling goes down. So I pretty much had it in my mind that I was going to have surgery.

"My answer was I have to have the surgery, and I didn't want to if I could beat the odds, I was going to do everything in my power to do that. I had another check-up after the first of the year, I went home, I went back to the gym, got my weight back up. I put about 30 pounds back on, went back into the doctor January 5 and a miracle. They were dumbfounded. They couldn't find any signs of any problem in my stomach; it's a miracle to me. I actually had to go back to the doctor yesterday before I came out here to get another CT scan on my stomach 'cause I still can't believe it."

Lesnar was asked if there were any risks to his return to fighting.

Saying that doctors had cleared his return, Lesnar added, "No, not at all. I've had three or four different opinions. I've had colonoscopies done, the CT scans, there's literally no sign of anything even existing in there. I believe the mind is a powerful thing and just every day I was put in a position I had to view my life and the world in a different way, I had a different take on the world. When you have everything taken away from you and you're laying helplessly in your hospital bed, not sure if I'm going to get back in the Octagon, something I've grown to love to do—this is my life.

"I've always been in control. I've been in control of my life, I've been in control of my surroundings, and for me...for 15 or 30 days not having control of anything, let me tell you, I've got to thank my wife and my family for sticking by my side, Dana and the UFC, and my sponsors. These people put everything on the line for Brock Lesnar."

White, who accompanied Lesnar in the interview with ESPN, said Lesnar's illness "did shake up the UFC. You know, first and foremost, I was worried that this guy was going to have a completely different quality of life. You know, the surgery he was looking at having...but he's healthy, and obviously I'm ecstatic."

White said he expected Lesnar to return in the summer of 2010, adding the return could come as early as May 29 in Las Vegas. When healthy, White said Lesnar would fight the winner of the upcoming fight between Frank Mir and Shane Carwin. If either of those fighters were injured, another possibility was a fight with Cain Velasquez, who defeated Nogueira at UFC 110 in Sydney, Australia, on February 21. Velasquez defeated Nogueira by KO at 2:20 of the first round.

Lesnar told ESPN, "I'm feeling 100 percent. I haven't felt like this for almost a year and half. I've had to get back and work my way back up because I lost a lot of weight. Listen, when I left the hospital, the next day I was in the gym. I was doing a little cardio, little sauna, just to get the sweat going. And some weights. I've had to work up from ground zero. I've actually had to build my base up again. And now I'm damn near right there. I'm alive and well, and I'm still the UFC heavyweight champion and ready to kick some ass."

Lesnar, who changed his diet and regained all of the weight he lost during the illness, told the Associated Press, "I think it's [the diet that] raised my condition level because I was really at the bottom. Now I'm back in the gym, and I feel great. I feel like my old self again. The heavyweight division should be back on their toes again."

Speaking with the *Minneapolis Star Tribune*, Lesnar said, "I'm doing all the right things. I'll be back in the gym [tomorrow] morning, and I'm going to have a minicamp and get ready for the winner of...I'm getting ready for anybody and everybody. I know the heavyweight class, the heavyweight division [is] definitely back on their toes because Brock Lesnar is back."

Las Vegas Review-Journal columnist Ed Graney wrote about Lesnar's comments, "Well, at least the time away didn't ruin Brock Lesnar's appetite for controversy. This can be a good thing for the Ultimate Fighting Championship. You can market a despised heavyweight champion as much as a beloved one. Lesnar will test that theory more than any fighter in UFC history. He is healthy enough to fight again, which on the surface is good news for a sport that has been missing some of its stars and suffering at the gate. In a weird, twisted way, this is part of why he is the sport's biggest draw. He is Notre Dame football to the mixed martial arts fan. Love him. Hate him. People pay to watch Lesnar. You can't discount the power of an entertaining heavyweight champion."

Just as Lesnar was returning to the public eye, the *Wrestling Observer Newsletter* published its 30th annual readership awards in its February 1, 2010, issue. Even though his year was interrupted by illness, Lesnar was prominently mentioned in the awards, taking first place in several categories.

Lesnar was the top choice—for the second consecutive year—as the Mixed Martial Arts Most Valuable. The newsletter summarized, "Lesnar was the most talked about fighter [UFC welterweight Georges St. Pierre was second] of the year, even though he only had one fight. He won the award by being the biggest drawing card in MMA history, with his match with Frank Mir headlining UFC 100 and drawing an estimated 1.6 million [PPV] buys, the fourth highest total in the history of PPV."

For the second consecutive year, Lesnar was also named Best Box Office Draw (over John Cena of the WWE). Lesnar was third in the Most Charismatic category (Cena was first, and Jeff Hardy was second).

One heavyweight looking forward to Lesnar's return was Mir. In mid-February, Mir told a Pittsburgh radio station that he wouldn't mind a rematch with Lesnar.

"I hate who he is as a person," Mir said in the interview. "I want to break his neck in the ring. I want him to be the first person that dies due to Octagon-related injuries."

A week later, after White had called Mir "an idiot" for his comment and called the incident "unprofessional," Mir issued an apology through the media.

"I would like to apologize to Brock Lesnar, his family, the UFC, and the UFC fans for my stupid remarks," Mir said. "I respect Brock, all the other fighters, and the sport of mixed martial arts. I'm sorry that I stepped out of line."

Lesnar told MMAweekly.com that he'd be more than happy to fight Mir again.

"Absolutely," Lesnar said. "I'd be delighted to fight Frank again. You know what? I don't think I beat him as bad as I could."

In an interview with KFAN radio in Minneapolis, Lesnar downplayed Mir's remarks.

"It was out of line, but in the fighter's mentality I don't want to go in the Octagon and kill somebody, but I want to do whatever I can to win," Lesnar said. "Maybe that's what he was saying. I don't know. The guy should probably just focus on the task in front of him, which is Shane Carwin, because if Shane Carwin beats [him], he won't be fighting me."

On March 25, the UFC and THQ, Inc. unveiled UFC Undisputed 2010. Lesnar was the featured athlete on the cover of the video game. Lesnar, who also had a clothing line, certainly understood the business side of the UFC.

In an interview with *UFC Magazine* in the fall of 2009, Lesnar said he had learned the business side during his time in the WWE. "I'm an athlete. But I understand that it's gonna take more than that for people to want to buy my pay-per-views. This is a business. The WWE sells big fights. The [Vince] McMahon family has been doing it for many years. I learned a lot as far as interviewing and talking in front of the camera. All this stuff that I'm doing now, except the fighting, is old news to me. But more important is understanding the business side of things. I love fighting. I wouldn't do this if I hated it. [UFC fighters] are not forced to fight. But you better make a little money out of it. To fight just to say that you did it is a pretty crazy thing to do. It is a hazardous job; I take it very seriously."

On March 27, 2010, Lesnar was in attendance at UFC 111 in Newark, New Jersey, and learned who his opponent would be when he returned to the Octagon. Lesnar saw Shane Carwin, who was fighting for the first time in more than a year (he was Lesnar's scheduled opponent when Lesnar got sick), knock out Frank Mir at 3:28 of the first round and earn the UFC interim heavyweight title. It was the first time Carwin, who improved to 12–0 with seven KOs and five submissions, had defeated a Top 10 fighter as a UFC fighter.

"The time off has given me basically a year of technique to work on," Carwin told the Associated Press several days before the fight.

USA Today reported that the "hype had already started" for the Carwin-Lesnar fight. "Lesnar came into the cage to face off with Carwin, congratulating him on the fight but saying the belt was 'make believe.' Carwin replied that he'll be ready for his chance."

The Carwin-Lesnar bout, which would unify the UFC heavyweight championship, was tentatively scheduled for UFC 116 on July 3 in Las Vegas.

"I think everything works out for a reason," Carwin told *MMAWeekly Radio* in early April. "That's probably the reason right there. Getting that win over Frank, that's two of Brock's five fights. So being able to fight Frank and get to Brock for that just put me into title contention.

"One thing that hurt me was sitting out. I was supposed to fight Cain [Velasquez] and they moved that, then they bumped me to Brock, obviously people had questions about that. In the mean time, I've been sitting out waiting to fight Brock or Cain, and all these other guys were fighting and still winning. So that makes their records and them look like a better contender, so I think at this point it was best that I fought Frank.

"That's one thing that [Lesnar] does well, and I think he obviously studied that part of the game for a while when he was doing the WWE stuff, so it probably comes natural to him, but like I said, that stuff I actually find pretty amusing. If they come out and they rip on me, or comment, I'll actually have a laugh about it. That kind of stuff doesn't affect me. I want to be remembered as the type of fighter for my fights in the Octagon, not for all the talk outside of it."

Lesnar was established as the early odds-on favorite by Las Vegas oddsmakers to defeat Carwin, who had not had any of his 12 fights go past the first round.

On May 4, 2010, the Lesnar-Carwin fight was officially announced in a press release from the UFC. The unification bout was scheduled to be part of UFC 116, which was scheduled for July 3, 2010, at the MGM Garden Arena in Las Vegas.

"When people wonder why the heavyweights capture the imagination of all fight fans, it's because of guys like Brock Lesnar and Shane Carwin," UFC president Dana White said in the release. "Not only are they great athletes and former national wrestling champions, but they both have the ability to end a fight with one punch. This is one of those fights you won't be able to turn away from because it can be over in a split second, and when it's over, only one will walk away as the undisputed UFC heavyweight champ of the world."

In the same release, Lesnar said he was eager for the fight. "I can't wait to get back in the Octagon and defend my UFC heavyweight title. July 3rd can't come soon enough. I'm ready to fight at UFC 116; Shane Carwin is going to face the real UFC heavyweight champion. I'm going to end Shane's perfect record and walk out of the Octagon with my championship belt around my waist."

Carwin said he was looking forward to the fight, as well. "I have wanted a chance to compete against Brock since my college wrestling days. He is an elite athlete who is always dangerous. His college wrestling background makes him extremely tough. I will be the first fighter he has faced who is his equal in size. He won't be able to bully me or hold me down as he has others in the past. This is the biggest fight of my life. I think it can go down as one of the greatest fights in UFC history. I expect to have my hand raised to become the real UFC heavyweight champion."

Coincidentally, on the same day that the Lesnar-Carwin fight was announced, Strikeforce and M-1 Global announced that Fedor Emelianenko, the top-ranked MMA heavyweight, would fight UFC and Pride veteran Fabricio Werdum in San Jose, California, one week before the Lesnar-Carwin fight on June 26, 2010.

CHAPTER 10

BORN TO FIGHT

Less than a year after his UFC debut, Lesnar was the UFC heavyweight champion and the promotion's biggest pay-per-view draw.

Shortly after his victory over Randy Couture at UFC 91 in November 2008, Lesnar told the Associated Press, "I'm done bouncing around trying to figure out what I want to do with my life. [MMA] has been everything I hoped for and more."

Lesnar's agent told the Associated Press, "This is what Brock was born to do. He's not the Next Big Thing anymore. He's the Big Thing."

In 2009, Lesnar told interviewers that he had found his calling. A week before he got sick, Lesnar told Dan Wetzel of Yahoo! Sports, "This is who I am. I'm a fighter."

Away from the UFC and wrestling, Lesnar and his wife, Rena, had found a stable, quiet life.

———

Rena Mero and Lesnar had started dating in 2004 after she was divorced from Marc Mero. Rena Mero had left the WWE in August 2004. She and Marc Mero had gone to work for WWE in 1996 and Rena, wrestling under the name Sable, became one of the best known WWE Divas. In 1998, she won the women's championship. She left the WWE in June 1999 but returned to the organization in 2003.

Rena and Lesnar became engaged in 2004, but the engagement was called off in early 2005. They became engaged again in January 2006 and were married on May 6, 2006.

In 2008, Lesnar and his wife moved to a 40-acre ranch near Alexandria, Minnesota—a town of 11,000 about 120 miles northwest of Minneapolis. In Alexandria, Lesnar was able to be close to his daughter from a previous relationship (born in 2002). In June 2009, Rena gave birth to a son.

Brock's college wrestling coach understood Lesnar's move.

"I think in the end, his roots are small town," University of Minnesota coach J Robinson said in a 2009 interview. "You know, everybody kind of wants [fame] until they live it, and then they realize that you can't go anywhere. Everywhere you go there are people bumping into asking for this, asking for that. And everyone thinks it will be great until it happens to them and then it's not so cool.

"I have a friend [who's] a writer, John Irving. He lives in upstate Vermont. Away from the hustle and bustle of everything. You go back and get away from it. The point being is that people like that, have so much notoriety that they artificially have to get away from it. You know, go to a small town. Paul Newman, same way, lived in Connecticut. In Connecticut, it was just 'Paul, how are you doing?' That's what people want. I think everybody wants to be successful, but everybody doesn't want notoriety. There's a difference. And that's why I think people do that, so they can go on and live as normal a life as they possibly can. And then when they need to step into the spotlight to do what they do, they do it. And they have the ability to step out of it."

Lesnar told *Sports Illustrated* in March 2009, "Up here people let you lead your life. Even if you're the Britney Spears of Alexandria, it means you might have to sign one autograph on your way to go ice fishing."

In Alexandria, Lesnar worked out in his own private gym with sparring partners on his payroll.

"Everything here is mine," Lesnar told *Maxim* magazine in 2009, "It's a controlled environment. I don't have to have people in here [who] I don't want around."

> ## "I think everybody wants to be successful, but everybody doesn't want notoriety. There's a difference."
> —Coach J Robinson

One of Lesnar's sparring partners was UFC fighter Chris "The Crowbar" Tuchscherer, who had an 18–2 mixed martial arts record as of February 2010. At UFC 109 on February 6, 2010, Tuchscherer won a majority decision over Tim Hague. The 6'1", 260-pound Tuchscherer, a native of Rugby, North Dakota, was a two-time NCAA Division II All-America selection for Minnesota State University–Moorhead.

Tuchscherer had tried out for the 10th season of *TUF* but was turned down. A week after being turned down, he received a fight contract offer from the UFC.

In an interview with Cagepotato.com, Tuchscherer talked about how he got started working with Lesnar. "I met Brock two and a half years ago at Minnesota Martial Arts Academy when I was working out down there, and shortly after that he signed a UFC contract and called me up to be one of his workout partners. I live in Fargo, North Dakota, which is only 90 miles from where he lives, so I basically travel down there for the week when he's preparing for a fight and come home on weekends."

Tuchscherer was asked what it was like to be a "human punching bag for the UFC's heavyweight champ."

"A human punching bag? No, I don't feel like that at all," he said. "I feel like ever since I've started out with Brock, I've helped him with his game, and he's helped me with mine."

Tuchscherer was then asked about facing Lesnar in a UFC fight one day.

"I've never thought about it," Tuchscherer said. "I'm just happy to be where I'm at right now. I'm in the moment, and I'm ready to fight and see where it goes."

In an interview with another website, MMAMadness.com, Tuchscherer summed up training with Lesnar, "We got a solid group of guys that have been together for the last couple of years. It seems like we've got things working for us right now."

Another UFC fighter traveling to Alexandria to work out at Lesnar's camp was Jon Madsen, a former high school nemesis of Lesnar's. Madsen, who handed Lesnar two of his three losses during his high school senior season, had started training in MMA after his college career at South Dakota State. Madsen, who won an NCAA Division II championship and was a three-time All-America selection in college, was featured on the 10th season of *The Ultimate Fighter*. At UFC 112 in the United Arab Emirates in April 2010, Madsen scored a unanimous-decision victory over Mostapha Al Turk to remain undefeated in five UFC fights.

Another fighter serving as a training partner for Lesnar was a 6'4", 300-pound former Army boxer named Eric Prindle. During his 10 years in the Army, the 33-year-old Prindle, who was born in Erie, Pennsylvania, was a five-time All-Army champion and four-time Armed Forces champion.

In a July 2009 profile of Lesnar that appeared in the *Minneapolis Star Tribune* six days before UFC 100, Myron P. Medcalf wrote, "Although he's worth millions and has been one of the biggest draws in athletics over the past decade, he chooses to live like the J.D. Salinger of sports. Lesnar emerges once or twice a year to punch, kick, knee, and wrestle a pre-determined foe for a half-million bucks and extras that likely include a portion of the UFC's PPV revenue. The bulk of his time is spent in Alexandria."

Medcalf pointed out that Lesnar had not taken advantage of his UFC fame.

"Hollywood producers have called Lesnar's camp with dozens of offers, but he has turned them all down," Medcalf wrote. Medcalf wrote that Lesnar's UFC contemporaries like Randy Couture, Chuck Liddell, and Georges St. Pierre "had taken advantage of UFC's booming business."

Lesnar told Medcalf, "I'm not a big spotlight kind of guy, and if I was, I was probably faking it before. I'm content with my family and my life right now and the way my career is going. Nothing more. Nothing less."

Lesnar admitted to *Maxim* in 2009 that he had made mistakes during his WWE career. "When you get money and you've never had it before, maybe you want to show it off. I acted foolishly."

Medcalf wrote, "Lesnar doesn't bend when it comes to personal privacy. He won't let media snap photos of him on his ranch. He won't say what he named his newborn baby. His barber wouldn't talk about him because he hadn't gotten permission to do interviews. When he grabs a beer in Alexandria, patrons keep their distance, unless Lesnar invites them closer."

Lesnar told Medcalf that he had become a "homebody because he's had to deal with 'shady' people throughout his life."

John Schiley, Lesnar's high school wrestling coach, told Medcalf that as a kid Lesnar didn't gain support from many people, but when he became famous he had to stay in Schiley's basement to escape whenever he came home.

"There were people [who] didn't think much of him, who were his very best friends then," Schiley said. "But he knew the difference."

Lesnar, who had walked out on an interview with ESPN in 2008 when asked about steroids and has always maintained that he has never used performance-enhancing drugs, addressed the issue for Medcalf.

"I've taken every random drug test I possibly can," Lesnar said. "That must mean I've never taken anything."

In an interview with *Maxim* in May 2009, Lesnar talked about the ESPN incident. "My interview was over. And then all of a sudden, 'Oh wait, we've got a few more questions.' Then they ask me about steroids. I've never in my life tested positive for steroids. What do you want me to say? I bet you I've taken over 60 steroids tests. In college I had 15 random drug tests in two years. I've taken drug tests for the NFL, WWE, the UFC. I must be pretty good at masking steroids."

Wetzel wrote in October for Yahoo! Sports, "When not working at a nondescript training facility, he hunts and fishes. He drives rusted, used trucks. He doesn't have the Internet. If it weren't for an occasional hunting show and NFL football, he'd throw out his television. He couldn't be happier. He's found balance."

Lesnar told Wetzel, "Fighting is not my life. My family is my life. I know who I am and what I'm about. My wife knows who I am. My children know who I am. My friends. That's all that matters to me."

> # "The only thing that matters to me is that I'm happy and my family's happy."
> —Brock Lesnar

Lesnar told a teleconference before UFC 100, "I got the best job in the world. I get paid to train. I get paid to fight. I'm home with my family every night. I'm lucky, and I feel very fortunate. There's going to be jealous people. There's going to be people [who] want to be your friends, you know what I mean? But I don't give a damn what anybody thinks. The only thing that matters to me is that I'm happy and my family's happy."

In an interview with the December 2009 issue of *UFC Magazine*, Lesnar was asked if he would have wanted to compete in the UFC under the old rules.

"Sure, I think the rules suck," Lesnar said.

He said he disliked the current rules because "It's regulated so that we can be on television. But I don't know—it's a fight. There weren't any rules when I was fighting at the Sisseton [South Dakota] street dance, when I was getting bitten in the back of the neck and had a 2x4 welted over me. But no, who wants to watch that? This is entertainment. But someday it might evolve into that, who knows? And it might become wrestling and it might all become fake, like wrestling."

Asked to elaborate about the Sisseton Street Dance, Lesnar said, "It's just a dance where I learned for the first time in a fight that numbers really mattered. And I was outnumbered."

Asked what he wanted his UFC legacy to be, Lesnar responded, "At the end of the day, I just want to be able to go home and enjoy life and hunt and spend time with my family. Legacies...those are made-up things. What's my legacy? I don't know what my legacy is. My legacy is former NCAA champion/pro wrestler who failed to make [it] in the NFL [but] comes in and cleans house in the heavyweight division. Becomes UFC heavyweight champion. That's going to be my legacy."

When asked if he was concerned about how he would be remembered by fans, Lesnar said, "I'm not a very sentimental guy. At this moment in time, I can't even tell you where my UFC belt is. It's somewhere, but I'd have to ask my wife to get if for me because I wouldn't know where it is."

Lesnar said he did know "where all my deer stands are, probably. And I know what my daughter likes to eat. I think I know my wife. I hope I do. As far as materialistic things, no, I'm not living in a material world."

Asked to look into in the future (the interview was written before his illness), Lesnar said, "When I first got into this, I told my wife, 'Just let me do three fights.' But now it's become a whole beast of its own. Now I'm just one fight at a time. I've got a new contract. I don't see the end in sight for quite some time."

CHAPTER 11

RETURN TO THE OCTAGON

Lesnar's illness in the fall of 2009 caused many to wonder if his fighting career was over. Lesnar was worried about more than just whether he would step into the Octagon again.

"I felt like I was on my deathbed," Lesnar told a conference call before UFC 116. "I really did because I was very sick. This illness, it kills a lot of people. And it's one of those things that I never even knew I had. Everything was up in the air because I'd lost so much weight."

For almost three months, Lesnar's career was on hold because of what was eventually diagnosed as diverticulitis. But after two weeks in the hospital and recovery, Lesnar was given the okay to resume workouts.

"I wasn't sure if I really wanted to fight again," Lesnar said of that period while he was hospitalized. "I thought I was going to have major surgery and have part of my colon removed and that would've been a two-year process for me to even come back on. So I really feel like I got—like I'm a cat with nine lives. I've got, I think I've got about eight left."

After resuming his workouts, Lesnar revamped everything—diet, training, and conditioning.

"I think the setback for me actually has been a good thing because it allowed me to sit back and really focus on my diet, the way I trained," Lesnar said. "I really regrouped and kind of rejuvenated myself. So I took a new approach on it as far as training and everything. And it's been very refreshing, and I've really come leaps and bounds. It's been a great thing. I'm excited to fight."

Lesnar conceded that when he resumed training in January, "I knew I had some obstacles in front of me."

The biggest obstacle was regaining weight and strength and getting back into fighting condition.

One of the first things Lesnar did after resuming training was bring in a new strength and conditioning coach and a new boxing coach. Lesnar said he brought in the coaches, "Just to evolve. Things were getting a little stagnant. Just to change things up and take a new approach on how can I become better? How can I get better? You've got to go back to the drawing board. I really went back to the drawing board on life when I was sick.

"I had to focus on a lot of different things. I mean my family first and my friends and all these other things. And when I originally got down and decided that I was going to…that I could fight and continue this legacy, I thought, 'You know what, I've got to make some changes. I want to get better. When I come back I want to be in greater shape. I want to be a better fighter.' And so that was the main reason for the changes."

A smaller obstacle when Lesnar resumed training was that he didn't know who his next opponent would be. In early May, it was announced that Lesnar would fight Shane Carwin, whom he had been scheduled to fight in November before his illness. On March 27, Carwin won the UFC interim heavyweight title by knocking out Frank Mir.

The unbeaten Carwin, a former college wrestler who hadn't had a UFC last past the first round, is almost a physical mirror image of Lesnar—6'2", 265 pounds with big hands. To prepare for Carwin, Lesnar worked on improving his standup skills. One way did this was by sparring with the bevy of big fighters in his training camp.

"You know, my camp is full of big guys," Lesnar said. "I've got [former University of Minnesota heavyweight] Cole Konard, who's a two-time NCAA champion. Chris Tuchscherer [who also was on the UFC 116 card], who's a runner-up Division II wrestler. Jon Madsen, who's a national champion in Division II, and [former NCAA champion] Marty Morgan."

In addition to those fighters, Lesnar brought in a wrestling/MMA legend to help prepare him for Carwin.

"I recently had Randy Couture in my camp," Lesnar said two weeks before UFC 116. "So I've been surrounded by greatness, I believe. And I believe that's what you have to do, you have to surround yourself with people that are going to push you."

Lesnar said the chance to work with Couture, whom he defeated for the UFC heavyweight championship at UFC 91 (on Nov. 15, 2008), was beneficial.

"Absolutely," Lesnar said. "Randy Couture is the godfather of this sport. I mean you've got your Royce Gracie and all these other guys, but these guys aren't fighting any more.... Randy's a once-in-a-lifetime kind of guy. I mean he's 45 years old, and he's still fighting. I brought him here, and I was very impressed with Randy, how he trains, and how he just...he's 45 years old and this guy comes in and he's a grinder, man.

"He taught me a lot of different things this week, last week. There's a lot of tricks to the trade, and Randy's one of those guys [who] wasn't always the biggest guy but he fights very smart. And being able to fight him and win the belt from him and have him come into the camp and say, 'You know these are the things you do great and these are the things I think you can do better.' It was very refreshing. But not—here's the most important thing—when Randy Couture comes into your gym, you have to raise your intensity level. It's one of those things where he just brings his ambiance into the gym and everybody that's in there raises their game. And that's the most important thing."

After his long layoff, UFC observers wondered if Lesnar would be rusty. Lesnar told a pre-fight conference call he wouldn't be rusty.

"I've had about 40 tune-up fights in the last eight weeks in training camp," Lesnar said. "If I have any rust on me by the time July 3 rolls around, it's a crying shame."

UFC observers wondered what type of fight the two former college wrestlers would produce. Carwin, who was 12–0 with seven victories by knockout and five by submission, told the pre-fight conference call that he was ready for any type of fight.

"I can see the fight taking place everywhere," Carwin said. "I've prepared in all areas, and I'm just ready to get in there and fight it and do what I love to do, and this is fun for me."

Lesnar agreed the fight could go either way. "I think this fight could either stay on its feet or it can go to the ground," Lesnar said. "Any way this fight goes it's going to be exciting. Shane poses different things that I haven't faced. Shane poses some different threats that I haven't had, one being the size and strength and the wrestling.

"Shane's heavy-handed, and you know he's a Division II national champion wrestler. You've got knockout power, so we've trained to avoid, you know, there's things that we want to do and there's things that we want to avoid. And so it's really simple. He's got a heavy right hand, and he's a strong guy."

Lesnar acknowledged the two fighters had taken different paths to UFC 116.

"He's got 12 fights," Lesnar said. "I just took a different route. I got thrown to the wolves right away where Shane's been able to get out and cut his teeth a little bit. And where I was thrown into the cage right away and had to fight big fights right away. So every fight's a big fight. It's whether or not you're prepared for them or not. And I believe that I am."

Lesnar concluded by saying that he was just happy to be fighting anybody, even if that fighter happened to be unbeaten.

"I'm just excited to get back in the Octagon. I don't give a damn who it is," Lesnar said. "I'm just...I'm excited to fight. You know the thing about records and knockouts, and this, that, and the other thing— you can't pay any attention. Because anything can happen once the Octagon closes and the only thing you have control [over] is your training camp and you know you go into these fights to be the best prepared that you can possibly be.

"There's always that puncher's chance of things happening, but you want to prevent all those things and you know you're in control and you're kind of not at the same time. You want to be offensive and defensive and, you know, try to come out on top. And, that's what we've trained for."

Carwin said in the pre-fight conference call, "If I touch anybody with my hands, I can knock them out."

Finally, the day for UFC 116 arrived. Lesnar was entering the Octagon for the first time in nearly a year since his victory over Frank Mir at UFC 100 on July 11, 2009.

In the first round of the fight at the MGM Grand Garden Arena in Las Vegas, Carwin's words about his hands almost proved to be prophetic. Carwin dominated the round and the fight almost ended in the first four minutes.

In the opening minute, Carwin withstood a takedown attempt by Lesnar and then stunned him with an uppercut that sent him to the ground. Carwin proceeded to pummel Lesnar with as many as 40 consecutive punches. Lesnar withstood the onslaught and, despite a cut over his left eye that was bleeding, managed to do just enough to prevent referee Josh Rosenthal from stopping the match. Lesnar was able to get back to his feet late in the round.

Lesnar's comeback continued in the second round. Early in the round, Lesnar took down Carwin and, once he had control on the ground, Lesnar locked up an obviously tired Carwin in an arm triangle choke hold. Less than a minute later—with 2:19 remaining in the round—Carwin was forced to tap out. The amazing comeback victory was Lesnar's first UFC victory by submission.

Carwin described the first round for www.ufc.com, "I was going after the kill. He's a tough SOB. I tightened up."

As for the submission, Carwin said, "I thought I had enough space to breathe, but he sunk it in tight, and I was going out."

"I just had to weather the storm," Lesnar said. "He's got some heavy shots. I knew he was getting tired. Each shot was less dramatic than the other."

After his victory over Frank Mir a year earlier, Lesnar had caused a stir with his post-fight comments and antics. Lesnar's post-fight behavior was much different this time.

Lesnar told the post-fight press conference, "It was just…he hit me pretty good and I didn't know for a second. I ended up on the ground and went into survival mode and just tried to stay busy. I thank the referee for allowing that thing to go on. I wasn't hurt, I thought if I just kept moving. I could feel Shane's punches slowly becoming less and less. I thought, 'If I can get out of here, then I can exert a bunch of energy.' I realized there was a short time left [in the first round], I just tried to stay busy. He's a beast. He definitely won the first round."

Lesnar credited his training and experience for being able to regroup. "Well, I've been in those situations before," Lesnar said. "I think some of my pro wrestling days prepared me for the ups and downs of things. I don't get too emotionally attached to a certain round, you know. We train for that in the gym. There are certain things that are going to happen, and you have no control over them. You just do whatever you can to get out of that and do the right things to move on. I knew I lost the first round, but there were still four rounds to go. I knew we were in a fight, for sure [and] here we go."

Lesnar had worked on the submission hold in his training.

"We kind of suspected that he would be prepared for my ground and pound," Lesnar said. "This submission [was pointed out to me as] something very feasible [for me] to do. Basically, it's just a headlock. We just trained for it. It's great."

Lesnar summed up the last 12 months.

"It's just great to win," Lesnar said. "Honest to God, I mean, after what I've been through since November of 2009 up until this point, it feels like it's been 10 years. It's been a grueling, grueling road. I can say, I mean, until someone actually can say they saw me.... Marty Morgan was by my side at my hospital bed from day one and saw me. To be where I was and to be here, really, truly is a miracle. It is. To come back from all that and to be here, words just can't describe it. I feel like I'm in a dream."

Lesnar added, "I stand before you a humble champion."

After the post-fight press conference, Lesnar jumped on a private jet for the flight back to Minnesota, where his wife was in the final weeks of a pregnancy.

Carwin, who was taken to a hospital immediately after the fight, released a statement on his Twitter account the day after the fight: "What happened to me July 3rd is called 'Lactic Acidosis.' It was brought on by a few things and mainly not breathing while exerting energy. I was all cramped up, nausea and major headache. Let me be clear, Brock won the fight, no issues that he earned the right to be the champion. Just passing on the info as it comes 2 me. I will fight him any time I get the chance."

One opponent neither Lesnar nor Carwin would be fighting soon was Fedor Emelianenko, who was beaten by Fabricio Werdum in San Jose, California, one week before UFC 116. It was Emelianenko's first loss in 10 years.

One week after the fight, the UFC announced that Lesnar's next opponent would be Cain Velasquez. The fight was expected to be on October 23 in Anaheim, California, as part of UFC 121. Velasquez had an unbeaten 8–0 record after defeating Antonio Rodrigo Nogueira at UFC 110 in February 2010.

APPENDIX

BROCK LESNAR ATHLETIC HIGHLIGHTS

Webster (South Dakota) High School

1992–93—Finished first at the District 1B tournament at 152 pounds. Finished second at the Region tournament. Qualified for the Class B state meet. Compiled a 22–17 record.

1993–94—Finished fourth at the Northeast Conference meet at 160 pounds. Finished third at the District 1B tournament and third at the Region tournament at 160 pounds. Qualified for the South Dakota Class B state meet, where Webster finished second as a team. Compiled a 28–13 record.

1994–95—Finished first at the Northeast Conference meet at heavyweight. Finished first at the District 1B tournament at 189 pounds. Finished second at the Region tournament. Placed third at the South Dakota Class B state meet, where Webster finished third as a team. Compiled a 38–4 record.

1995–96—Finished first at the Northeast Conference meet at heavyweight. Finished first at the District 1B tournament at heavyweight. Finished first at the regional tournament. Placed third at heavyweight at the South Dakota Class B state meet, where Webster finished second as a team. Compiled a 34–3 record.

Bismarck (North Dakota) State College

1996–97—A 23–5 record, placed fifth at heavyweight at the NJCAA national meet.

1997–98—A 33–0 record, placed first at heavyweight at the NJCAA national meet.

University of Minnesota

1998–99—Compiled a 24–2 record with eight pins. Had a 21-match winning streak. Won Big Ten Conference heavyweight title and finished second at NCAA Championships.

Match-by-match:

January 9, 1999, Great Plains Invitational: dec. Corey Stevenson, Iowa State, 6–0; dec. Mike Dixon, unattached, 5–3; dec. Matt LeBlanc, St. Cloud State, 7–1; lost to Trent Hynek, unattached, 5–3.

January 16, 1999, National Duals: pinned Ben Bauer, Augsburg, 0:50; pinned Jack Leffler, Central Michigan, 1:52; pinned Wes Hand, Iowa, 2:36; pinned Todd Munson, Oklahoma State, 3:54.

January 22, 1999, dual meet: pinned Matt Brink, Michigan, 2:20.

January 23, 1999, dual meet: dec. Matt Lamb, Michigan State, 11–3.

January 30, 1999, dual meet: dec. Wes Hand, Iowa, 6–0.

January 31, 1999, dual meet: pinned Jason Pernat, Wisconsin, 1:34.

February 5, 1999, dual meet: dec. Karl Roesler, Illinois, 9–2.

February 7, 1999, dual meet: dec. Eric Wood, Ohio State, 14–5.

February 12, 1999, dual meet: dec. Matt LeBlanc, St. Cloud State, 11–0.

February 14, 1999, dual meet: dec. J.R. Phenis, Nebraska, 7–5.

February 19, 1999, dual meet: pinned Jacob Vercelli, Purdue, 2:52.

Appendix

March 6, 1999, Big Ten Championships: pinned Jake Wade, Indiana, 1:06; dec. Jason Pernat, Wisconsin, by default; dec. Matt Brink, Michigan, 12–2.

March 7, 1999, Big Ten Championships: dec. Karl Roesler, Illinois, 7–0.

March 18, 1999, NCAA Championships: dec. Sean Hage, West Virginia, 12–2; dec. Bronson Lingamfelter, Brown, 0:22.

March 19, 1999, NCAA Championships: dec. Derek Delporto, Slippery Rock, 4–0; dec. Leslie Apedoe, VMI, 10–2.

March 20, 1999, NCAA Championships: lost to Stephen Neal, Cal State Bakersfield, 3–2.

1999–2000—Compiled a 31–1 record with 15 pins. Had a 22-match winning streak. Won Big Ten Conference heavyweight title and finished first at NCAA Championships.

Match-by-match:

November 13, 1999, Bison Open Invitational: pinned Aaron Vogt, Ridgewater C.C., 1:10; pinned Dustin Darveaux, unattached, 1:17; dec. Garrett Lowney, Minnesota, 3–2.

November 19, 1999, dual meet: pinned Dave Clymer, North Dakota State, 2:47.

November 28, 1999, dual meet: dec. Dustin Darveaux, St. Cloud State, 15–4.

November 28, 1999, dual meet: dec. Matt Eberle, Hofstra, by forfeit.

December 10, 1999, dual meet: dec. Paul Hynek, Northern Iowa, 10–2.

December 12, 1999, dual meet: pinned Joe Slaughter, Portland State, 1:24.

January 7, 2000, dual meet: pinned Matt Zutavern, Nebraska, 0:39.

January 9, 2000, dual meet: pinned Dave Anderton, Oklahoma State, 3:48.

January 14, 2000, dual meet: dec. Mark Janus, Penn State, 10–6.

January 15, 2000, dual meet: pinned Tony Sylvester, Ohio State, 0:51.

January 22, 2000, National Duals: pinned Damion Martindale, Montana State–Northern, 0:31; dec. Seth Charles, Cornell, 4–1; dec. Dave Anderton, Oklahoma State, 13–3.

January 23, 2000, National Duals: dec. Mark Knauer, Iowa State, 11–3.

January 28, 2000, dual meet: pinned Justin Staebler, Wisconsin, 2:02.

January 29, 2000, dual meet: dec. Michael Dixon, Indiana, 7–1.

February 7, 2000, NWCA All-Star meet: dec. Bandele Adeniyi-Bada, Penn, 5–4.

February 11, 2000, dual meet: pinned Matt Brink, Michigan, 3:26.

February 13, 2000, dual meet: dec. Matt Lamb, Michigan State, 6–4.

February 18, 2000, dual meet: pinned Josh Saul, Northwestern, 1:15.

February 20, 2000, dual meet: lost to Wes Hand, Iowa, 5–3.

March 4, 2000, Big Ten Championships: pinned Michael Dixon, Indiana, 2:31; dec. Mark Janus, Penn State, 8–1; dec. John Lockhart, Illinois, 2–1.

March 5, 2000, Big Ten Championships: dec. Wes Hand, Iowa, 2–1.

March 16, 2000, NCAA Championships: dec. Bart Johnson, Boise State, 4–2; pinned Shawn Laughlin, Lehigh, 2:18.

March 17, 2000, NCAA Championships: pinned Tim Courtad, Ohio, 4:04; pinned Bandele Adeniyi-Bada, Penn, 6:41.

March 18, 2000, NCAA Championships: dec. Wes Hand, Iowa, 3–2, tiebreaker.

Ohio Valley Wrestling

Won Ohio Valley Wrestling Southern Tag Team Championship (with Shelton Benjamin) three times.

February 13, 2001: defeated the Disciples of Synn.

May 15, 2001: defeated the Disciples of Synn.

October 29, 2001: defeated Rico Constantino and The Prototype John Cena.

Appendix

WWE

Championship Match Results

August 25, 2002—At Uniondale, New York, defeated The Rock.

November 17, 2002—At New York City, lost to The Big Show.

March 30, 2003—At Seattle, defeated Kurt Angle.

July 27, 2003—At Denver, lost to Angle.

September 18, 2003—At Raleigh, North Carolina, defeated Angle.

February 15, 2004—At San Francisco, lost to Eddie Guerrero.

MMA

June 2, 2007—At Los Angeles, defeated Min-Soo Kim, first round
(1:09) submission.

UFC

Feb. 2, 2008—UFC 81 at Las Vegas, lost to Frank Mir, first round
(1:30), submission.

Aug. 9, 2008—UFC 87 at Minneapolis, defeated Heath Herring, third
round (5:00), unanimous.

Nov. 15, 2008—UFC 91 at Las Vegas, defeated Randy Couture for
UFC heavyweight championship, second round (3:07), TKO.

July 11, 2009—UFC 100 at Las Vegas, defeated Mir to defend UFC
heavyweight championship, second round (1:48), TKO.

July 3, 2010—UFC 116 at Las Vegas, defeated Shane Carwin for UFC
heavyweight championship, second round (2:19), submission.

BROCK LESNAR'S WRESTLING MOVES

(from www.onlineworldofwrestling.com)

Finishing Moves: The F5 (also known as The Verdict) and Shooting Star Press (during OVW career).

Other favorite moves: The Brock Lock (Sitting Leg Muffler), The Brock Lock (Bearhug during OVW career), Superplex, Backbreaker, Knee lift to gut, Overhead belly-to-belly suplex, Triple non-release powerbomb, and Running Corner Shoulderblock.

Notable WWE feuds: The Hardy Boyz, Bubba Dudley, Ric Flair, Rob Van Dam, The Rock, The Undertaker, Kurt Angle, Shelton Benjamin, Charlie Haas, John Cena, Zach Gowen, The Big Show, Chris Benoit, Hardcore Holly, Eddie Guerrero, Bill Goldberg, and Steve Austin.

PROFESSIONAL WRESTLING GLOSSARY

Babyface: A good guy.

Dark match: A non-televised match that is part of a televised show. It is usually used to test new talent or warm up the crowd for the televised portion of the show.

Diva: Used by the WWE to refer to any woman involved in wrestling.

Feud: A battle between wrestlers or promotions. In the WWE, a feud usually lasts several months.

Heat: Negative crowd reaction.

Heel: A bad guy.

Kayfabe: Term used to describe the illusion that professional wrestling is real.

Turn: When a wrestler switches from babyface to heel or heel to babyface.

Undercard: Matches preceding the main event on a card or show.

ACKNOWLEDGMENTS

I would like to thank Scott Rowan of Triumph Books for giving me the opportunity to work on this project. Scott was the project's biggest supporter and helped me overcome some obstacles. I would also like to thank Adam Motin and Karen O'Brien of Triumph Books for their patience and insight. I am also grateful for the help the following people provided to this project: Lou Babiarz of the *Bismarck Tribune*; Dee Bertsch, Buster Gilliss, and Carolyn Twingley of the Bismarck State Athletic department; former Bismarck State wrestling coach Bruce Basaraba; Jeaneen Bingner of the South Dakota High School Athletic Association; South Dakota State University wrestling coach Jason Liles; Pat McCabe and Jeff Keiser of the University of Minnesota athletic media relations staff and University of Minnesota wrestling coach J Robinson; Sandy Date, Jeff Day, Myron P. Medcalf, and Michael Rand of the *Minneapolis Star Tribune*; Webster (South Dakota) High School athletic director William Sawinsky; John and LeAnn Suhr of the *Webster Reporter and Farmer*; and Traci Wagner and Theresa Walenta of the University of Iowa athletic media relations office. There are numerous websites devoted to pro wrestling, mixed martial arts, and the UFC. One web site was a continuous source of information and insight about all three—F4Wonline.com.

SOURCES

BOOKS

Couture, Randy. *Becoming The Natural: My Life In and Out of the Cage* (New York: Simon and Schuster, 2009).

Keith, Scott. *Dungeon of Death: Chris Benoit and the Hart Family Curse* (New York: Citadel Press, Kensington Publishing Corp., 2008).

Shields, Brian and Kevin Sullivan. *WWE Encyclopedia* (New York: DK Publishing, 2009).

Wertheim, L. Jon. *Blood in the Cage: Mixed Martial Arts, Pat Miletich, and the Furious Rise of the UFC* (Orlando, Florida: Houghton Mifflin Harcourt, 2009).

DVD

WWE Home Video: *Here Comes the Pain,* 2003.

OTHER PUBLICATIONS

Maxim

Pro Wrestling Illustrated

Sports Illustrated

UFC Magazine

University of Minnesota: Wrestling media guides from 1999, 2000, 2001, and 2010.

WEBSITES

www.cagepotato.com

www.cnnsi.com

www.dakotagrappler.com

www.espn.com

www.examiner.com

www.f4wonline.com

www.gophersports.com

www.jrsbarbq.com

www.kayfabememories.com

www.lordsofpain.net

www.mmaacombatzone.com

www.mmamadness.com

www.mmascraps.com

www.mixedmartialarts.com

w3.nexis.com

www.onlineworldofwrestling.com

www.ovwrestling.com

www.reporterandfarmer.com

www.sdhsaa.com

www.sherdog.com

www.sportsnet.ca

www.startribune.com

www.ufc.com

www.usatoday.com

www.yahoo.com

www.youtube.com

www.wikipedia.com

www.wrestlingnewsworld.com

www.wrestlingworld.com

www.wwe.com

ABOUT THE AUTHOR

Joel Rippel, who has worked for newspapers—including the *Orange County (Calif.) Register* and *Minneapolis Star Tribune*—for nearly 30 years, is the author of four books on Minnesota sports history. He lives in Minneapolis.

INDEX

Index

Index

Index